DEFENSIVE PISTOL

FUNDAMENTALS

GRANT CUNNINGHAM

Published by

Gun Digest® Books, an imprint of F+W, A Content + eCommerce Company
Krause Publications • 700 East State Street • Iola, WI 54990-0001
715-445-2214 • 888-457-2873
www.krausebooks.com

To order books or other products call toll-free 1-800-258-0929
or visit us online at www.gundigeststore.com

Cover photography by Yamil Sued

ISBN-13: 978-1-4402-4280-9
ISBN-10: 1-4402-4280-1

Cover Design by Dane Royer
Designed by Marilyn McGrane
Edited by Corrina Peterson

Printed in USA

CONTENTS

FOREWORD 4
ACKNOWLEDGEMENTS 5
INTRODUCTION 7

PART 1: FIRST THINGS FIRST
CHAPTER 1 Safety First! 15
CHAPTER 2 Being Efficient 17

PART 2: THE HARDWARE: YOUR PISTOL AND HOW IT WORKS
CHAPTER 3 Picking a Semi-Auto Pistol 24
CHAPTER 4 Ammunition for Defensive Shooting 47
CHAPTER 5 Testing Your Pistol for Reliability 53

PART 3: THE CONCEPTS YOU NEED TO KNOW
CHAPTER 6 Realities of Defensive Shooting: The Ambush Attack 62
CHAPTER 7 Your Body's Natural Reactions 72
CHAPTER 8 Making Decisions Efficiently 81
CHAPTER 9 What is Precision in Defensive Shooting? 90
CHAPTER 10 Balance of Speed and Precision 101
CHAPTER 11 Can You - Or Should You? 112

PART 4: THE SKILLS YOU NEED TO LEARN
CHAPTER 12 Managing Scarcity: What Skills Do You Need? 120
CHAPTER 13 Foundations - Grasp and Stance 126
CHAPTER 14 Trigger Control - The Key to Efficient Shooting 136
CHAPTER 15 Eyes and Sights - The Defensive Sighting Continuum 146
CHAPTER 16 Drawing the Pistol 160
CHAPTER 17 After Shooting - Assess! 171
CHAPTER 18 Dealing with Multiple Aggressors 178
CHAPTER 19 Reloading Your Pistol in an Emergency 183
CHAPTER 20 Malfunctions - What They Are and How to Deal With Them 197

PART 5: PUTTING IT ALL TOGETHER: TRAINING AND PRACTICE
CHAPTER 21 Integrity in Training 205
CHAPTER 22 Training in Context 213
CHAPTER 23 Choosing a Training Course 217
CHAPTER 24 Practicing Realistically: Drills and Procedures 224

APPENDIX A Respectful Irreverence 244
APPENDIX B An Alternate Look at Handgun Stopping Power...... 247

FOREWORD

By Rob Pincus, I.C.E. Training Company

G rant Cunningham is one of the most articulate and discerning voices in the world of defensive shooting. There are louder voices, there are voices that you may hear more often, there are voices backed by longer resumes and there are voices that speak with first hand combative knowledge… but, his is a voice that I recommend you listen to with the highest priority. In fact, there isn't anyone in the industry today that I think provides you a better opportunity to learn about defensive handguns and their use under the stress of lethal threat. Surely, there are many voices worth listening to on these and other personal defense topics, hopefully mine is included, but you're holding a unique resource in your hands.

If you're familiar with my work through television, training DVDs, Personal Defense Network™, articles or you've actually trained with me on a range, you'll recognize many of the concepts and principles that Grant shares in this book. Grant is not only a certified Combat Focus® Shooting Instructor, he is also one of the leaders in our community. While I am cited as the "developer" of the Combat Focus® Shooting Program, the truth is that our team of instructors (and our students!) have contributed much to the evolution of CFS over the last decade. Whether it has been their questions, their comments, their problems or their solutions, scores of other people have been responsible for the tweaks, leaps and changes that make CFS what it is today and will be in the future. Looking back over the past handful of years, no one has pushed our team forward, or helped us overcome hurdles, more than Grant Cunningham. Whenever I have a new concept, explanation or drill that I want to vet through for the program, Grant is one of my go-to guys. Even outside of CFS, when I am working on any project related to personal defense firearms, I count on Grant's guidance, experience and insight to spot check my own thinking and/or to help me express my thoughts more clearly.

When Grant asked me to write the foreword for this book, I was honored, as you might expect. Naturally, I asked to review a copy of the book prior to writing it. After reading it, I am now humbled as well by the inclusion of many of our CFS concepts. This is a book that I wished I had written… but, the truth is that I couldn't have. Grant has a way of explaining concepts and sharing ideas that escapes me most of the time. I am simply not patient or thoughtful enough. It is his ability to communicate complex information elegantly that truly distinguishes his voice from the cacophony of "experts" that flood (sometimes very good, sometimes not so good) information into the shooting world in torrents of hyperbole, assumption and grammatical disaster.

This is a book that my mom can learn from, my daughter can learn from and that Navy SEALs coming home from deployment should read. All three stand to learn a great deal about Defensive Pistol Fundamentals. This is not a book about "shooting" and it's not a book about "guns"… it's a book that will help anyone be better prepared to defend themselves or those they care about with a semi-automatic pistol. When it comes to the true fundamentals of defensive pistol shooting, it's probably the best book ever written.

Rob Pincus, May 2014

5/2016

www.icetraining.us

PS- Read My Book Next!

ACKNOWLEDGEMENTS

You may think a book is a solo effort, that the words spring forth from the author's mind without need for any other human involvement, but you'd be dead wrong. Like a movie, there's more going on than just the stars on screen; a lot of talented people come together in any endeavor such as this, and I'm privileged to know some of the best.

When I wrote my first book I gave primary credit to my wife, and she still deserves it. Behind every good man stands a woman, and my case is no different. Were it not for her patience and support I doubt I'd even bother writing.

Rob Pincus graciously wrote the Foreword and allowed me to reprint his superb essay "Respectful Irreverence" in the Appendix. Rob has made defensive shooting, and teaching defensive shooting, his life's work. Through constant questioning and evolution he's worked his way to the top of the training business, inspiring and influencing many along the way. When we met some years ago I was surprised how closely our views meshed, and though we have occasional divergence of opinion it's fair to say that a lot of my current approach to the subject has been affected and shaped by his work.

Massad Ayoob is the man most responsible for my career as a writer, for it was he who brought my name to the general public more than a decade ago. When it comes to the judicious use of lethal force I doubt there is anyone who knows more about the subject than Mas; I'm grateful that he gave of his valuable time to review the section on legalities and supply much-needed feedback.

Greg Ellifritz of Active Response Training, a career cop with a penchant for research, graciously allowed me to reprint his groundbreaking article "An Alternate Look at Handgun Stopping Power" in the Appendix. He surprised many in the shooting world when his data showed that what we thought were tremendous differences between the various calibers and cartridges simply didn't exist. I'm grateful that he agreed to share that article with you.

My colleague Paul Carlson at Safety Solutions Academy was a great help in helping me distill some of my ideas into usable forms. Paul is one of the few people in the defensive training business who is innovative and forward-looking, and is developing a following because of his iconoclastic approach to teaching critical skills.

The models in the photographs come from my personal contacts, and their selfless time given to play both good and bad guys really makes the illustrations work. In no particular order, my heartfelt thanks go to Jacq Shellito, Brenden Shellito, Jason Ault, Jennifer Krug, Aaron Jenks, Carl Fitts, Grant

Fitts, Maurice Rahbani, Georges Rahbani, Liliane Rahbani, Hoda Rahbani, and master gunsmith Todd Koonce (who has the singular distinction of appearing in every book I've so far written!)

Jim Jacobe of The Jacobe Group in Salem, OR, maintains a large pistol inventory for his students, which gives them the chance to try out different guns and see which fits them the best. Jim was kind enough to loan me several pieces from his inventory for the illustrations, saving me the expense of buying them myself.

Thanks also to Don Frederickson at Skyline Ford in Salem, OR, who provided some of the vehicles used in the pictures, as well as portraying an attacker in some of the scenario photos.

Finally, my editor Corrina Peterson and her team at Gun Digest have done a superb job taking my manuscript and turning into something actually worth reading. If you like this book, it's because of them! They're efficient, professional, and always a joy to work with. I'm lucky to have them on my side!

Grant Cunningham, June 2014

THE WORST-CASE SCENARIO
WHAT WE TRAIN FOR

Those who have chosen to arm themselves, whether in their home or legally on the street, face the prospect that someday, somewhere, they may have to shoot someone in justifiable self defense.

That's what this book is about.

Physical conflicts, as violence expert Rory Miller points out,[1] are idiosyncratic things; no two are alike. A lethal force incident is no doubt the pinnacle of all defensive encounters, but reason suggests that even at the top there is a hierarchy of severity, a scale of danger and our response to it.

It's possible to get into a shooting situation knowing ahead of time that you may have to shoot. The loudmouth who accosts you in the parking lot over a disputed space may escalate his actions from simple shouting to an assault with a deadly weapon. You may start with a conciliatory, concessionary posture all the while planning your response should things get worse. This type of encounter gives you some indication ahead of time that you might need to draw your pistol, giving you time to work out the details of your response in your mind. We're not talking about a whole lot of time, mind you, but enough to prepare for what might come, to be proactive in terms of your readiness to engage your attacker.

This kind of incident – the anticipated fight, or what Miller refers to as 'social violence' – is the easiest kind of incident (if any deadly force situation can be called 'easy') to prepare for precisely because you have some fore-knowledge of the circumstances under which you'll shoot. It is the kind of incident an awful lot of defensive shooting courses prepare their students to face because it lends itself to assembly-line training and choreographed drills.

An escalating incident takes time, has an aspect of mutual agreement.

The problem is that these kinds of incidents may also be the least common type of deadly force encounter that we're likely to face. Miller contends that attacks (as differentiated from fights) happen "closer, faster, more suddenly and with more power than most people can understand."[2] The surprise attack is the most difficult to anticipate and therefore the most difficult to defend. It's also, as it appears, very common.

The best database of private sector self defense shootings that I know of has been compiled by Tom Givens, the founder and co-proprietor of Rangemaster in Memphis, TN. Tom has had more verified students involved in defensive shootings than anyone else, and he's taken pains to document every one of them – over 60, the last time I checked. He's also appeared in a Personal Defense Network training video called "Lessons From The Street," where he recounts several representative cases from his files.

This work is unusual because the victims he interviews are people who have trained with him previously. Tom is a superb instructor, and it's safe to assume that his students are more aware and prepared for violence than the average person on the street. Yet they still became victims; the difference between them and the untrained victims common to the rest of Memphis is that Tom's students were able to fight back and win in all but two cases - and in those two cases the victims were not armed at the moment they were attacked.

The surprise attack, the ambush, is the worst-case scenario we'll be considering throughout this book.

Living your life leaves you open to many ordinary, everyday distractions which can be exploited by an attacker.

What might come as an eye-opener to many people is the fact that his students were almost always surprised by their attackers. There wasn't an overly extended eye contact period where the attacker and his prey were sizing each other up, or a protracted testosterone-fueled dance of one-upsmanship. The defenders were living their lives and minding their own business one moment, and in the next were faced with a life-or-death decision. This is how attacks happen, both for Tom's students and for us.

Note that I didn't use the word "fight." That word implies a certain level of voluntary participation by both parties and a certain level of anticipation. I use the word attack specifically because that's what happens: one person attacks another, who is forced to either defend or capitulate.

This book is about defending yourself from the surprise criminal attack, or the criminal ambush. It's about that very short period of time – measured in seconds – when you find your life in imminent danger and where lethal force is the correct response. It's also the most difficult kind of incident to prepare for and therefore is too rarely discussed in CCW or defensive shooting courses.

Imagine you're deciding between onion rings and french fries one moment, and the next you're forced to shoot someone to save your life. The surprise attack, the ambush, is the worst-case scenario we'll be considering throughout this book.

We focus on the ambush because the skills necessary to go from zero expectation of lethal force to actually shooting a second or two later are very different from those needed when you can see it coming and have the opportunity to get ready. This is reactive shooting in its truest sense, and is routinely ignored in much of the defensive instruction currently available.

WITHOUT WARNING: SKILLS ON DEMAND

If you knew that you were going to need to shoot someone in the next 20 or 30 seconds, your brain would have some time to decide what it was going to do, what neurons it would fire and in what order, to accomplish the task[3] of causing your attacker to stop. Your brain would prepare your body to act.

If on the other hand you're attacked without warning or expectation, your brain doesn't have that time to get ready, to pre-tense muscles and get into its fighting stance. Your body's natural and instinctive reactions, happening as they do without cognitive thought,[4] will be your first indication that something is wrong. The effectiveness of your response has a lot to do with how efficiently you convert those instinctive reactions into responses, and is something that you don't need to do when you have some amount of early warning.

Skills that are applicable for those instances when you have preparation time – getting into just the right stance, holding the gun just so, and finding the perfect sight picture – usually go right out the window when the threat has suddenly appeared in your face. Now you don't have the right stance or the right grip and perhaps can't even see your sights clearly. What good are those finely honed skills when you can't employ them because the situation has exceeded their utility?

On the other hand, if you practice skills that are applicable to the ambush attack, skills that work when you don't have time to get yourself ready, you'll be prepared to deal with this worst-case scenario. What's more, those skills will still work at that lower level, in that kind of incident where you do have a little time to see the attack coming and think about it.

The target shooter's stance, with perfect alignment and positioning, doesn't often happen – if it ever does – in reactive defensive shooting.

Response to a predatory ambush looks very different from the target shooting or competition stance.

THE WORST-CASE SCENARIO

That's why this book will deal with the worst-case scenario: the sudden, chaotic, and threatening criminal attack. We'll look at how the body reacts in those cases, how to work with the body's natural reactions, and how to train realistically to convert those instinctive reactions into intuitive responses.

In this book we'll be limiting the discussion to attacks that occur beyond about two arms' reach. Why such an arbitrary distance? First, because most attacks happen outside of that limit,[5] and second, because the skills needed inside that range are more dependent on things other than shooting. Those inside-of-two-arms'-reach skills are certainly important, and I recommend that you take a class in dealing with them, but in most of the cases in which you're likely to need to employ your pistol you'll be farther away – typically up to about a car's length away. (Sometimes, of course, the ranges will be a little longer, but Given's research shows that his students experienced 86%

Data show most defensive shootings occur between three and five yards, or beyond two arms' reach.

Most defensive shootings happen outside of two arms' reach; inside that range a different range of skills is needed.

of their encounters between three and five yards. That's where we'll start, because that's where you're most likely to need your skills.)

The first section of this book deals with the hardware itself: how to shoot it, carry it, reload it, and manipulate it. This book is focused on pistol han-

The author teaching a Combat Focus® Shooting class.

dling from the defensive point of view, as opposed to hunting or target shooting. I'm interested in the most efficient, error-resistant methods I can find to protect my life and the lives of my students, and that's what you'll find here. Every aspect of how to handle the pistol has been evaluated not for how well it works in a shooting contest, but how well it's likely to work when your hands are shaking and sweating because someone is trying to do you harm.

The first section, then, is concerned with **how** to operate the pistol.

The second section deals with the concepts of defensive shooting: how attacks happen, how your body reacts to a lethal threat, how you process information about your attacker, and so on. We'll talk about what precision is (and isn't), the need to know about your own balance of speed and precision in defensive shooting, and a little bit about the legalities and ethics of using lethal force against an attacker. These are the principles on which the skills you'll learn are based; they are the things that affect **how** and **what** you train.

In the third section we'll look at the skills that both work against a surprise attack and work with your body's natural reactions to that threat, or how to use the pistol to protect your life or the life of your loved ones. (These two sections contain information based in part on the Combat Focus® Shooting (CFS) program from I.C.E. Training, for which I'm a certified instructor.)

Why these specific skills? Primarily because they're built on science and observable fact. We start with the realities of how attacks happen – not the way we wish they'd happen or the way television tells us they happen, but how objective evidence tells us they do. We must take into account the science behind our natural threat reactions, the medical evidence and research into how we survive violent attacks.

The responses that we choose – the 'tactics', in modern parlance – must work both with the reality of the attack and with what our bodies do in relation to being threatened. That's the basis of what you're going to learn in these pages: responses that work well with what our bodies do, naturally, when threatened. If you can do things that work with your body, rather than against it, doesn't it stand to reason that those will be both more effective and more efficient than those that don't?

Understand that this is not a Combat Focus® Shooting manual. There are many concepts in a CFS class that we won't touch on in this book, and there is material in this book which is congruent with CFS methodology and philosophy but isn't part of the official curriculum. I encourage you to take a Combat Focus® Shooting class (whether from me or one of the other Certified Instructors) in order to get the full experience.

Finally, the last section puts it all together and talks about how you should train, how you should pick a training course, and how you should practice for maximum results within the limits of your training resources. It also addresses how you approach your training, and how to avoid short-circuiting your training.

I hope you enjoy and profit from what is to come!

---

[1]Miller, Rory: "Meditations on Violence", ISBN 1594391181

[2]Miller, Rory, "The Four Basic Truths of Violent Assault". http://www.budoseek.net/vbulletin/content.php?147-The-Four-Basic-Truths-of-Violent-Assault

[3]Maimon, G. & Assad, J.A.: Parietal Area 5 and the Initiation of Self-Timed Movements versus Simple Reactions. The Journal of Neuroscience, 26(9), 2487-2498

[4]Angell, James Rowland, "Reflex Action and Instinct". http://www.brocku.ca/MeadProject/Angell/Angell_1906/Angell_1906_o.html

[5]Givens, Tom: "Lessons From The Street" DVD, Personal Defense Network (2012)

CHAPTER 1

SAFETY FIRST!

Firearms are dangerous things – that's why we use them to protect ourselves and our loved ones. It is precisely because of the danger they pose that they make good tools to stop bad people from doing bad things to good people. That is, if they're used properly.

Used improperly, however, they present a danger to their user or to innocent people. That's not what we as conscientious, competent, law-abiding gun owners wish to have happen and why we approach all handling of firearms with safety first and foremost in our minds.

Guns always pose the same amount of danger, but the risk (the chance of that danger affecting us) changes. We make that change in risk happen with safety rules and procedures. Those rules and procedures ensure that the benefit we get from handling or using the gun outweighs the risk.

For instance, shooting a pistol makes an extremely loud sound and poses a very real danger to your hearing. You reduce the chances of that happening – your risk – by wearing good hearing protection. By doing so you will reduce the risk well below the benefit you'll get from shooting that gun, whether that benefit is simply recreational or preparation for saving your life.

For any drill that you do, or any class that you take, the benefit of doing or taking it has to outweigh the risk involved.

We reduce the risk of ear damage by wearing hearing protection – even if we're just a spectator.

Whether I'm teaching a class or simply handling a gun, I reduce the risk to myself and the people around me by following, and making sure everyone else follows, these easy-to-remember rules:

1) Always keep the muzzle pointed in a generally safe direction whenever possible. (A generally safe direction is one where, should the gun inadvertently discharge, it will not hurt you or anyone else. This changes from environment to environment, and requires that you always think about where the safe direction **happens to be.)**

2) Always keep your trigger finger outside of the triggerguard until you are actually in the act of firing. (The preferred place is straight along the frame above the trigger.)

3) Always keep in mind that you are in control of a device that, if used negligently or maliciously, can injure or kill you or someone else. (This means that you must always think about what your target is, where your bullets will land, and all the other things that could result in your gun causing human suffering.)

Safety is your most important responsibility. Whenever you pick up a gun, think about what you're doing and why. Reduce your risk, and help those around you reduce theirs by teaching them these rules.

CHAPTER 2

BEING EFFICIENT

As I mentioned at the beginning, this book is about dealing with the threat that you didn't know was coming: the criminal surprise attack – the predatory ambush.

If escape is impossible or impractical, your number one concern when you're attacked becomes getting your attacker to stop what he's doing. The sooner that happens, the better for you (and ironically, the better for him too). The key is to make the best use of your defensive resources to cause the bad guy to go away as soon as possible.

What kinds of defensive resources do you have? Time is certainly a major resource, and the less of it you use relative to the goal of making him stop the better. Time isn't the only resource, however; ammunition is certainly one, because you only have so many rounds in the gun and/or on your person. Your strength and energy are resources too, and even the space around you can be a resource.

To be efficient in terms of defensive shooting means to make the best use of those resources, or to put it another way, to use as little of them as you can to stop your attacker.

MORE EFFICIENT DOESN'T NECESSARILY MEAN FASTER

It's important to understand the difference between speed and efficiency, and it's common to confuse the two. Doing something faster would certainly seem to be more efficient, and very often in the defensive shooting community the words are in fact used interchangeably.

Speed is an isolated measurement, meaning that it is independent of conditions. Something is faster, something else is slower, and the measurement isn't concerned with the reason for the speed to exist, let alone for being measured.

Efficiency, on the other hand, is dependent on the reason for event; you can't make better use of your resources without knowing what they're being used to do. You're using resources to accomplish something, to reach some sort of goal, and it's only when that something is being accomplished or you're getting closer to the goal that you can determine if you've made the best use of your resources. Efficiency, as we'll use it in this book, is using the least amount of the resources at hand in order to achieve your goal.

Think about this: if you were in your car and your goal was to get to your destination as efficiently as possible, would that mean driving as fast as you could all the time? Of course not; driving faster not only uses more fuel (drag increases with the square of the speed), but it also increases the risk of accidents, traffic tickets, and parts breakage. If you wanted to be efficient you'd look at the shortest route, keep your speed as steady as possible, and make a good compromise between travel time and fuel usage – and, of course, obey the speed limits to avoid being stopped.

Efficiency, in other words, depends on the context: the circumstances under which something can be fully understood or applied. (You're going to hear more about context in the rest of the book.) Efficiency comes down to making the best use of resources considering the conditions under which they'll be used.

EFFICIENCY IN A DEFENSIVE SHOOTING CONTEXT

The context is what makes evaluating and understanding efficiency in defensive shooting difficult for a lot of people. Let's look at efficiency relative to a task you'll no doubt practice often: reloading your pistol during an attack.

If your only criteria for evaluation of any reload technique were speed, you'd start by using some sort of a timer to measure how long the entire process – or even parts of that process – take. Since the goal of measuring speed is simply to get faster, you'd likely find yourself changing the way you manipulate the pistol, how and where you carry your spare ammunition, how you look at the gun to guide your hands, and all sorts of other things large and small to gain even a slight reduction in the time it takes.

Let's take the same task of reloading the pistol and look at it from the standpoint of efficiency: making the best use of your resources under the conditions of their use. You'd first consider what might be happening when you need to do that reload. We'll talk about the body's natural reactions to a threat stimulus in a later chapter, but here's a good illustration of how they affect what you train: the fastest technique may be less reliable because your natural threat fixation has you watching the bad guy and not your gun; your fine motor skills have degraded, making them shaky and fumble prone; you're moving, which means your carefully staged positioning becomes impossible; it's dark and you really can't see what you're doing; your ammunition isn't in exactly the same spot you trained with; and so on.

The efficient reload technique takes into account those conditions and the goal itself. The efficient reload technique would reduce (or, preferably, eliminate) the need to look at the reload because it's harder to do so; it would make less use of small muscle groups and fine motor skills whenever possible, because those skills are degraded; and so on. The efficient reload method is chosen after recognizing and considering all those things that make it more difficult, and working around them to get to the goal more reliably. Reliable things are by nature efficient because they reduce potential hangups and bottlenecks.

Efficiency is determined by environment

Every aspect of your technique is affected by the environment and circumstances of the attack. You can train under some of them, but others (the body's reactions) you can only study and simulate their effect on the technique. Unless you consider both approaches in your training you'll make the wrong choices: you'll choose speed over efficiency.

Efficiency takes into account the goal: making the bad guy go away with minimum amount of resources at your disposal. Referring back to the reloading example, since the goal has conditions, an efficient reloading procedure takes into account all of the stuff in the environment, stuff that you wouldn't bother with if speed were the only objective.

For defensive purposes, you need to take into account all of the things – including your body's reactions to the threat – that might affect the successful completion of the reload. Once you've identified what is efficient, speed will take care of itself through practice.

Don't try to be faster; focus on being more efficient.

Consistency is a big part of efficiency

A large part of efficiency is consistency: doing things in the same place and in the same way as much as possible. In the context of the attack, consistency reduces the number of conditional branches (decisions) that your brain has to make to mount a response.

Efficiency applies to the training process, too. You have only so many resources – time, money, energy – to devote to your training. Consistency reduces the number of things that you have to practice, allowing you to make better use of your scarce training resources.

Think of it as recycling: the more times you can repeat specific movements or use specific concepts, the more repetitions you can get into any particular practice session. The more repetitions you get, the more imprints you make in your memory. The more imprints, the easier it is to remember and to recall them.

Consistency isn't the absolute, carved-in-stone, be-all and end-all of efficiency, of course. There may be times where the most efficient method isn't absolutely consistent with everything else. In those rare cases I hold to the goal of overall efficiency over sheer consistency. Exceptions are uncommon, however, and consistency is usually a good barometer of what is most efficient. If you're doing something that's inconsistent, or you're asked to believe in something that isn't consistent, there has to be a very cogent explanation of how it is more efficient. Usually there isn't one.

EFFICIENT AND EFFECTIVE AREN'T THE SAME, EITHER

Let's say that you've managed to find yourself in a situation where you really need to shoot an attacker. You panic, draw your pistol and start launching rounds in the general direction of the bad guy, firing from the hip or without actually looking at your target. Those rounds go all over, maybe hitting the miscreant – or maybe not, and you don't really know. Are you being effective?

Of course you are – at some level, anyhow. Even if you don't hit the guy you may cause him to seriously reconsider his chosen profession; he might cower and run away. Even if he doesn't do that, you've certain impacted his ability (and desire) to present a lethal threat to you. Yes, you've been effective – but you certainly haven't been terribly efficient, having used more ammunition, time, and energy than you needed to in order to achieve your goal of making the bad guy stop. Stop he did, but you didn't make particularly good use of your resources to make it happen. Those kinds of antics may not even reliably stop the bad guy.

Simply launching uncontrolled rounds at an attacker may or may not be effective – but it certainly isn't efficient!

Purposeful shooting style is both efficient and more effective.

Let's replay that scenario, and instead of panicking this time you quickly draw your pistol, sidestep as the gun extends out into your line of vision, drop into a physically strong natural stance and quickly place several accurate shots into his upper chest – at which point he collapses, ending his attack. You've certainly been effective, and judged objectively you've been more effective than in the first scenario. However, the main point is that you've been more efficient: you made the best use of your time, ammunition, and energy to make the bad guy go away faster. Your response was also far more reliable in effect. Your increased efficiency made you more effective, not the other way around.

Efficient things are effective things, but effective things are not always efficient.

**Sometimes a particular gun (or any other piece of gear)
isn't optimal for the job of defensive shooting.
That doesn't mean it's a "bad" gun, only that it
may not be optimal for the job you want it to do.**

In this book we'll focus on efficiency, because that's the best path to effectiveness. Remember that efficiency only exists in relation to a goal: in this case, stopping the bad guy during his attack on you. If you focus on making the best use of your defensive resources (time, effort, ammunition, space) to make the bad guy go away, you'll be effective. If you only focused on effectiveness, you wouldn't necessarily get your attacker to stop his activities before you ran out of some resource (time, energy, ammunition, or space).

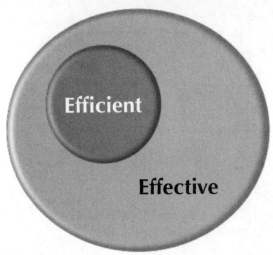

Things that are efficient are also effective, but not everything that is effective is necessarily efficient.

Things that are efficient are by definition effective, because you can't achieve a goal without effectiveness. If you focus on efficiency, effectiveness takes care of itself – because if you haven't been effective you can't meet the definition of efficient.

EFFICIENCY ALSO INVOLVES YOUR EQUIPMENT

There is some gear that is demonstrably more efficient than other gear. In the chapter talking about pistol actions I'll go into this in a little more depth, but a good example is how your firearm (and how you carry it) affects your efficiency. For instance, a gun that has more operational controls or more complicated functions will take more training time and effort, more practice time in maintaining proficiency, and will require you to do more (or remember more) things during a conflict where you need to use that gun. All of those are forms of inefficiency that derive from the hardware choice.

Some guns, just by nature of their design or form, force you into using less effective techniques. In the chapter on grasp and trigger control I talk about what an efficient grasp looks like and why it functions as it does. There are certain guns, however, that often (though not always) interfere with an ideal grasp and force the shooter into a grasp that's less efficient – meaning a grasp that results in lesser control of the gun and/or requires more effort in training or practice to maintain. If the gun forces you into a physical position that affects how precisely or quickly you can shoot, it's imposing an inefficiency on you.

Sometimes it's hard to admit that the gun (or any other piece of gear) isn't optimal for the job of defensive shooting. That doesn't mean it's a "bad" gun, only that it may not be optimal for the job you want it to do.

Focus on being efficient. If you truly understand that concept, it will lead you to automatically adopt both techniques and equipment that are effective.

CHAPTER 3

PICKING A SEMI-AUTO PISTOL

The first handgun I bought as an adult was a used Smith & Wesson Model 59, a traditional double-action/single-action pistol that was once quite popular. I purchased it in the late '80s from a local Sheriff's deputy who had upgraded to a new gun. It was in very nice condition, something of a rarity for police duty pistols, and came with a half-dozen "high capacity" magazines at a very reasonable price. He even threw in a shoulder holster!

Though an accomplished shooter and hunter with a rifle, I was handicapped by not knowing a whole lot about handguns (the only one my family had owned when I grew up was a little Ruger .22 Single-Six). I thought the imposing Model 59 would be the best choice for my wife and I to protect our home; after all, it was reliable, held a lot of ammunition, and must be a good gun because the cops used them. As the saying goes, it sounded like a good idea at the time.

The problem was that it wasn't the gun for either of us. Because of the double-stack magazine it was huge and my small hands could barely reach around the grips; the double-action-for-the-first-shot trigger was almost completely out of my reach, and even when in single-action mode I could just barely get a good hold and press the trigger. My wife fared a little better (her

There are many choices in semi-automatic pistols, but some are more suited to efficiently defending against an ambush attack than others.

fingers are longer than mine), but struggled with the heavy trigger on that first shot. We both had trouble using the combined decocker/safety, and the high bore axis meant appreciable recoil. (I won't bother to tell you about the gun not being "drop safe," which is why the Deputy was required to get a new version where that defect had been corrected!)

As it was, the choices in defensive autoloading pistols simply overwhelmed us and we picked something based on what someone else was forced by his employer to use. It wasn't a good choice, and we ended up getting rid of the gun in short order.

If you're like we were and new to the shooting world, or perhaps new to the semi-auto pistol world, the choices today are even more overwhelming. Aside from caliber choices, you have to decide on steel, aluminum, or plastic; hammer or striker; double action/single action (DA/SA), double action only (DAO), single action only (SA), or one of the newer "safe-action" types. It's enough to drive a person to drink!

It needn't be that way, though. By considering a few specific criteria it's actually pretty easy to wade through the myriad of choices in the pistol market and come up with the one that's right for you.

THE PISTOL HAS TO FIT YOUR HAND

No matter what size semi-auto pistol you buy, no matter what the caliber or action type, the pistol must fit your hand. A pistol that doesn't fit your hand is going to be more difficult to shoot well, less comfortable to shoot, train and practice with, and will negatively impact your ability to fully utilize its capabilities during an attack. If I had a choice between an optimum gun that didn't fit me and a second-tier choice that did (assuming they were equally reliable; more on that in a later chapter), I'd choose hand fit first.

Fitting the gun to you

How to decide if a pistol fits you? Start with a verified unloaded gun, and then ask another person to double-check its (unloaded) condition. Once that's been done, place your finger on the trigger so that the first joint of the trigger finger is on the face of, or just at the edge of, the trigger. That's generally considered the ideal placement for defensive shooting because it gives both good leverage and good control.

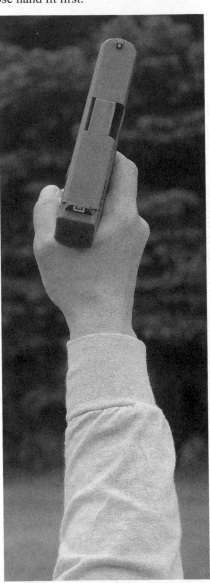

Once that's done, keep the trigger finger in that position as you wrap the rest of the shooting hand around the grip. Now, look at the direction the barrel is pointing relative to the bones of your forearm.

If the gun is too big for your hand, the barrel will be pointing away from the midline of your torso; for a right handed person, a too-big gun will point off to the right, for instance. You'll also probably notice that the backstrap of the gun's grip is pointed not at the fleshy part of your hand between your thumb and forefinger, but instead is pointed at the joint at the base of the thumb. This will result in a loss of control and the channeling of the gun's recoil force into that joint. That sounds painful, and it is! A gun that is too big for the hand is both more difficult and less pleasant to fire.

This gun is too big for the shooter's hand – notice how the barrel is not in good alignment with the forearm.

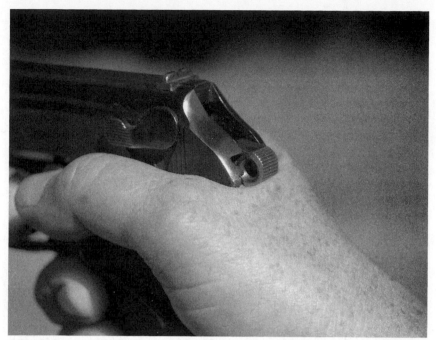

A gun that is too small, combined with a bit of excess flesh, can result in injury as the slide recoils.

The opposite condition, where the gun points in toward the centerline of the body, happens when the gun is small relative to hand size. This is actually a much easier condition to deal with than the opposite. In general, a gun that's slightly small doesn't present much of an issue; occasionally a very fleshy hand will have problems with lacerations caused by the recoiling slide, but in terms of the actual operation it's easier to deal with a too-small pistol than one that is too large.

In terms of the actual operation, it's easier to deal with a too-small pistol than one that is too large.

Operating the controls

Ideally all of the other major operating controls should be easily reachable with the shooting hand in its normal grasp. The magazine release, for instance, should be easily pushed with the thumb of the firing hand without unduly shifting your grasp.

The slide lock should also be in a position where you can engage it easily, should you need to lock the slide back to clear a malfunction (or for administrative purposes, like complying with range rules or cleaning).

For instance, I find that with my short thumbs it's difficult for me to operate the magazine release of most medium-sized autoloading pistols. The slimmer sub-compact models are generally not a problem, but getting into anything with a double-stack magazine makes it much harder to get a

You should be able to easily push the magazine release, preferably without shifting your grip much.

You should also be able to easily engage the slide lock without dramatic changes in your grip position.

consistent release. On the other hand, my wife has very long thumbs and can operate magazine releases that I find very difficult.

Check these fit points carefully on any pistol you're considering. If the gun doesn't fit well, no matter what its other attributes, it's probably not the gun for you.

WHAT KIND OF ACTION IS BEST?

The autoloading pistol world is a maze of operating systems and acronyms. Each system has its adherents, and you'll find no shortage of arguments as to their merits on any gun forum you wish to visit. Still, there are specific attributes to each which will affect how easy it will be to train and how efficiently you'll be able to engage your attacker.

Semi-automatic pistols come in two major forms: striker fired and hammer fired. Hammer-fired guns are perhaps the most iconic; like a revolver, they have an external hammer which is cocked, by the trigger in some systems, or by the thumb in others. For both, subsequent shots are usually cocked by the action of the recoiling slide. They will usually have a hammer spur, which is visible on the back side of the slide.

Striker-fired guns, by contrast, have a firing pin with a spring around it; when in the cocked position the striker spring is tensioned and, when the trigger is pulled, the spring drives the firing pin into the primer of the round in the chamber.

While there have been striker-fired pistols from nearly the beginning, it was Glock that made them popular in the modern age. Though still among the most popular police pistols made, companies like Springfield Armory (with their XD series) and Smith & Wesson (with their M&P) have made major inroads in the market and helped to make striker fired autoloaders the most popular type of defensive arms being sold. Though not generally issued by police departments, smaller companies such as Steyr and Walther have entered into the striker-fired pistol business as well.

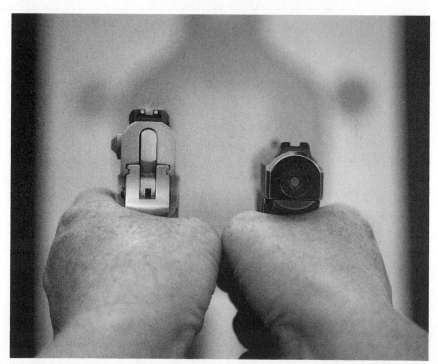

A low bore axis, such as the gun on the right, helps reduce muzzle flip and perceived recoil.

The advantage of the striker-fired pistol is usually a lower bore axis, meaning the bore of the barrel is closer to the web of the hand.

This reduces the perceived recoil of the gun, because the rearward force has less leverage than if it were higher up. I tell my students to imagine holding a vertical ruler in their fist, and pressing against it with a pencil. If you press toward the top of the ruler, any given amount of force will move the ruler more than that same amount of force applied closer to the hand. It works the same with recoil.

Hammer-fired guns, on the other hand, can offer cleaner, crisper triggers. If you want a very light and precise trigger, the hammer-fired pistol is the direction you look. That may not be a good choice for a defensive pistol, however.

TRIGGER STYLES

There are a surprising number of ways to trigger a shot in a semi-automatic pistol. Each of them has advantages and disadvantages, and in the realm of defensive shooting some are more important than others.

Single action (SA, S/A, or – rarely – SAO)

The single action is so named because the trigger does one thing and one thing only: releases a hammer that has already been cocked, either by hand or through the action of the slide. (There are, technically, some SA striker-fired guns, but their operation has far more in common with other actions than with the traditional, hammer-fired SA.)

The hammer-fired pistol's biggest advantage is the light, crisp trigger – but it has some disadvantages.

The Browning Hi-Power is a classic example of a single-action semi-automatic pistol.

The single action's biggest strength is the crisp and light trigger that requires little travel to break the shot. This makes it extremely easy to shoot; the downside, paradoxically, is that it can be too easy to shoot. The short, light trigger in hands that are already shaking from the body's natural threat reactions can be a bad combination, similar to having a cocked revolver in those same hands. It's too easy to inadvertently trigger a shot that wasn't specifically intended.

The single action requires some sort of safety to keep it from firing accidentally, and the manipulation of that safety – both off and on – must be practiced extensively if one expects to do so efficiently when faced with the prospect of one's own death (or grave bodily harm). That takes extra training time, effort, and ammunition and always holds out the possibility that you may forget something when stressed. (I've seen it happen in high-level simulations, and to some very good shooters. If you own a SA automatic, you have to be religious about training and practice!)

Double action (DA, DA/SA, or TDA for "traditional" double action)

A double action is one in which the trigger does two things in unbroken sequence – cock the hammer then release it to fire the shot. It's often called "trigger cocking," and that's a good term for it. Once that first shot has been fired, the action of the reciprocating slide cocks the hammer for you, and the rest of the shots are fired in shorter, lighter single action. If you stop shooting before you run out of ammunition, the hammer has to be lowered to a safe position; there is usually no safety to restrain a cocked hammer.

In most cases there is some sort of lever or button, called a "decocker," to lower the hammer safely; there are a few guns, however, where there is no such mechanism and the hammer must be lowered with the thumb while pulling the trigger on a live round. Try that when you're shaking because you've

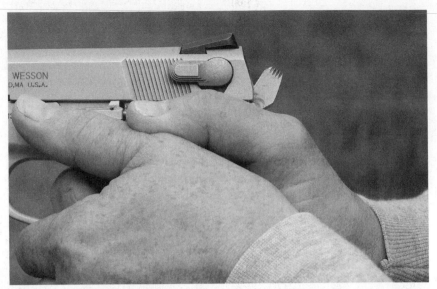

Traditional double-action guns are readily (though not always) identified by the presence of a decocking lever – in this case, on the slide of this S&W Model 3913LS.

been attacked! The decocker is another control that the shooter has to learn to operate in the proper order, and making it more complicated some decockers also serve as a safety to prevent that first double action shot. In those guns you have to train not just the operation of the decocker, but also the release of the safety before you shoot.

The transition from double action to single action can be difficult for some people. Just when you've gotten used to pulling the trigger through a long, heavy travel it suddenly gets much shorter and much lighter. I've seen this result in low first shots or high second shots, and it's pretty rare to find someone who can put both rounds in close proximity to each other when shooting quickly. It takes more training resources (time, energy, ammunition) to master the DA trigger than others; add into that the necessity to train in the operation of the decocker and, if applicable, the safety function of the decocker, and you can begin to understand why the DA is the most complicated pistol to use.

Most DA pistols are hammer fired, though there have been striker fired examples. Frankly, I've never been able to find a positive attribute to ascribe to the DA pistol for defensive use, though they sell in great numbers.

Double action only (DAO)

These guns operate like a revolver for every shot. The trigger cocks and releases the hammer, and on the next shot does it again. The long and heavy trigger remains the same for every round, and because the trigger takes some effort to manipulate there is, again like the revolver, no need for a safety. Since the hammer can't be cocked there is also no need for a decocker. These are among the simplest of all autoloaders to use.

A big downside of the DAO is that long, heavy trigger press. Like a revolver it takes some training and practice to really master, and can be a big issue for those with limited hand strength. Another issue is that DAO pistols are hammer fired, which means they tend to have a high bore axis and consequently greater perceived recoil.

"Safe action"

Though a trademark of the Glock company, this has come to be used generically to describe the action used by most modern, striker-fired pistols.

(Confusingly, the government's technical definitions for firearms result in some safe action guns being legally categorized as single action, and some being categorized as DAO. From the standpoint of the user, however, they are all very similar and for that reason will be grouped together.)

The safe action has a relatively short trigger travel and weight; shorter and lighter than a DA or DAO, but longer and heavier than a SA (or a DA that's transitioned to SA). The trigger is consistent in weight and travel; there is no transition from shot to shot.

A modern striker-fired pistol is generally easy to shoot; the triggers aren't hard to manipulate, they don't change, and the guns are generally considered to have no need for external active safeties that must be manipulated before firing. (There are some safe-action guns that do have external safeties, which many people – including yours truly – consider to be superfluous.)

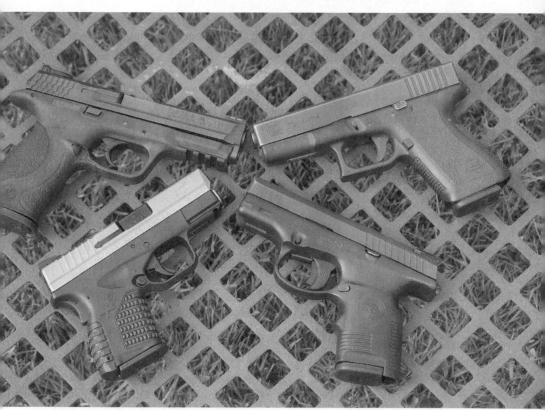

Models like these from Springfield, Smith & Wesson, Glock, and Steyr are examples of the modern, striker-fired pistols author recommends for self defense.

A modern striker-fired pistol is generally easy to shoot; the triggers aren't hard to manipulate, they don't change, and the guns are generally considered to have no need for external active safeties that must be manipulated before firing.

They are the easiest guns of all to train with due to their consistent triggers and lack of extraneous operational controls. Because of this they are also the most efficient: they require the least of your resources (time, effort, ammunition, and money) to achieve proficiency. These attributes have made the safe-action pistol the overwhelming favorite of police agencies and private citizens all around the country.

WHAT TO CHOOSE?

I recommend that your first choice be a modern striker-fired (AKA "safe action") pistol. Why? Because of their consistent operation, they're the easiest and most efficient to train with; they're the most efficient in use, due to their lack of extra controls; their striker-fired actions give the benefit of a lower bore axis and reduced perceived recoil; and they're available from many manufacturers in a wide range of sizes and capacities. Striker-fired guns are made in various sizes by Glock, Springfield Armory (the XD series), Smith & Wesson (the M&P), and Steyr (the "M" and "S" series). There are other manufacturers, but these are the guns I've used and can recommend without reservation.

In second place, though a ways back, I'd place the DAO pistols. They have the efficiency in operation of the safe-action guns, though they're a little harder to learn to use because of the longer, heavier triggers. Because they're hammer fired they also don't usually have the lower bore axis and recoil mitigation of the striker-fired guns. Still, on balance there's more positive than negative. Today the DAO genre is best represented by companies such as Kahr Arms, though other manufacturers such as Beretta and Walther may have some DAO models in their line.

Third place goes to the single-action autopistols. Their extra safeties require more training time and effort to master, and those light triggers mean that trigger finger discipline must be absolute. The user of a SA pistol must remember to practice defeating the safety as part of the draw stroke and remember to consistently apply the safety immediately after shots have been fired. New students (as well as quite a few experienced ones!) seem to find that a lot to remember, and it's hard for me to say that the benefits outweigh the issues.

Fourth place goes to the traditional DA pistol. I find little to recommend such guns; they require more training time to master two different trigger pulls plus the decocker, plus (on some guns) a safety as well. One-handed operation tends to be more difficult, as does consistent shot placement – especially at realistic speeds. Does this mean they're useless for self defense? Of course not; it just means that you'll spend more of your limited training resources in learning to use them safely and efficiently, and you'll require more practice in maintaining those skills. If you're truly committed to doing so, however, you'll still be ahead of those people who carry a gun for self defense and don't get any training or practice at all.

SIZE OF THE PISTOL: FULL, COMPACT, OR SUB-COMPACT?

If you're a normal-sized person, it's likely that you'll find more than one gun that fits your hand. (If you're short with small hands, like I am, you may not be so lucky!) Once you've found those gun(s) that your hands can live with, you'll need to consider the size of the pistol – because that affects concealability for carry, recoil, and even how precisely you can shoot.

Size ranges

There are no hard-and-fast rules for the category into which any given pistol falls. In general, a full-sized semiautomatic (often referred to as "service" or "duty" size) will have a barrel in the five-inch-long range, a grip frame that extends well below the hand, and will take the highest capacity magazines in the maker's line. Most such guns today have double-row (aka "double-stack") magazines, though older guns may be of the single-row style. Double stack magazines will often have capacities of up to eighteen 9mm rounds (this will

These Glock 9mm pistols show the progression from service-sized Model 17 to compact Model 19 to subcompact Model 26.

vary in states with magazine capacity limitations, of course). The Glock 17 is a good example of a full-sized pistol.

"Compact" (often called "carry") sized guns are usually just shortened versions of their full-sized brothers. The barrel length is reduced to around four inches (give or take), and the grip frame is slightly abbreviated to end at the bottom edge of the hand. The magazines, too, are shortened and have less capacity; instead of, say, 18 rounds of 9mm they may only have 13 or 14. The compact will almost always accept the longer magazine of the same-caliber service gun from which it is derived. In the Glock world, for instance, this would be a Model 19.

"Subcompact" guns are small pistols that may or may not be derived from a larger gun in the line. They usually have very short barrels (under, say, 3.5 inches) and correspondingly short grips that end within the space of the average hand. Capacities will drop to perhaps 10 rounds or so; in some cases, the subcompact model in a line will have a single-stack magazine in place of the double-stack used by its stablemates. The classic subcompact version of a larger model is the Glock 26 in 9mm.

Top: Full-sized Glock 17.
Middle: Compact Glock 19.
Bottom: Subcompact Glock 26.

This Springfield XD-s is a popular micro-sized 9mm pistol.

In recent years a new class of semi-automatic pistols has emerged: the "micro" pistol. These guns are small, light, and capable of being carried in a confined space such as a pocket, but are chambered for a standard defensive pistol caliber like 9mm (as opposed to the traditional "pocket gun" calibers like .32ACP and .380ACP). They are often smaller than what we would have considered normal for, say, a .380ACP pistol just a few years ago. They're invariably single-stack (for size and weight reduction) and of lowered capacity. Their main attractions are their diminutive size and weight.

Concealability

It should seem self-evident that the bigger the pistol, the harder it's going to be to conceal. What most people don't consider, however, is exactly what dimensions are important.

The hardest part of the pistol to hide is the grip; it's the part that usually sticks up and out, poking through covering garments to reveal the presence of the gun. The shorter and thinner that grip is, the easier it's going to be to hide (and the more flexibility you'll have in your wardrobe). In general, then, the lower the capacity of the pistol the easier it's going to be to conceal. It's usually easier to hide a pistol with a long barrel and a short grip than the opposite.

The length of the barrel is, in most concealment scenarios, somewhat less important than the size of the grip – but there are exceptions. If you're carrying with a belt holster, where the barrel is not contained within the waistband, the length of the barrel becomes more important. If you're relying on the length of a covering garment to hide the gun from view, then the length of the barrel does become an issue.

The thicker the gun is overall also dramatically affects how easy it is to hide. All other things being equal, the thinner single-stack pistols are generally easier to make disappear under clothing than their thicker, double-stack counterparts. Of course the tradeoff is in capacity: you'll carry fewer rounds in the pistol to get that concealment advantage. You have a decision to make.

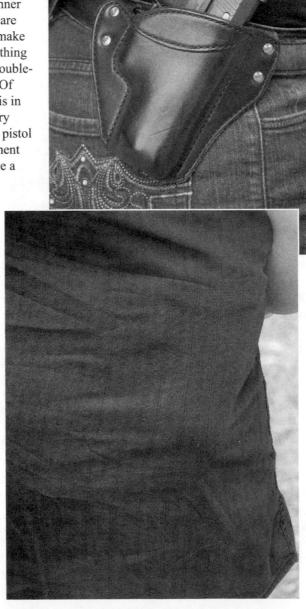

This pistol, with its fat grip, can be a challenge to conceal under light clothing.

Recoil control

The smaller and lighter the gun is, the harder it's going to be to control. That's just physics at work: the less mass the gun has, the more perceived recoil it's going to deliver and the more difficult it's going to be to shoot well. Every step down the size ladder, from full-size to compact to subcompact to micro, delivers progressively more felt recoil and becomes progressively harder to control. In other words, the size of the gun affects your balance of speed and precision (more on that concept in a later chapter).

For instance, many people (myself included) find the new micro-pistols very difficult – if not downright impossible – to control in realistic strings of fire, where a subcompact in that same caliber is easy and pleasant to shoot in comparison. Sometimes this makes the caliber choice harder: if you need the very small sized pistol because of limitations in how and what you can carry, but find that controlling the tiny guns in larger calibers is very difficult, you may have to make a compromise and get something like a micro-sized gun in .380ACP instead of 9mm.

The length of the barrel and grip aren't the only control issues. For any given size, a single-stack pistol is going to generate more pain in the hands than a double-stack of the same caliber. This is because channeling recoil force into the hand with a thinner grip means that the pressure per square inch is higher than with the wider grip, which distributes the same amount of force over a greater area.

How precise can you be?

The shorter the barrel and slide, the closer together the front and rear sights are. The closer they are to each other, the more difficult it becomes to align

Sight radius of full-sized Glock 17 is considerably longer than that of subcompact Model 26, making it easier to shoot to any given level of precision.

the sights properly. Sometimes referred to as "sight radius," this dimension can make a big difference in how precisely you can shoot with any given gun.

This doesn't mean that the shorter barrels aren't mechanically able to deliver rounds with less precision. In general, if you clamp a short-barreled and a long-barreled pistol into a machine rest and fire them you'll find that the shorter gun gives up no precision to its larger stablemate. However, the achievable precision, when the pistol is held in the hands and the sights are being aligned by a combination of visual acuity and motor skills, will usually be noticeably affected by the shorter barrel.

It's not a gun issue, it's a usability issue. Some people shoot the smaller guns very well and some don't. Before making a decision on a small pistol you should ideally shoot it against a larger version to determine where your limits for usability are.

CALIBER SELECTION

No discussion in the world of defensive shooting will cause more grief and heartache than one about calibers. Everyone has their own favorite, for good and sometimes not-so-good reasons, and everyone believes that their choice is the absolute best. Just like everyone else!

The major defensive pistol calibers – 9mm, .40S&W, and .45ACP – have terminal results that are very similar to each other.

Complicating matters is the fact that hard data is both difficult to come by and difficult to analyze. While there have been studies done, the conclusions drawn from the data presented are sometimes suspect as each camp twists the evidence to suit their own agenda.

At this writing, the best publicly available data and analysis I've seen has been from Greg Ellifritz at Active Response Training.[6] A career police officer, Ellifritz decided some years ago to collect the best data on defensive shootings that he could and then to look at the results dispassionately.[7] What he found delighted some, infuriated others, but along the way gave us what is, in my opinion, the most level-headed look at this notion of caliber effectiveness. (His groundbreaking article, "An Alternate Look at Handgun Stopping Power," is published in its entirety in the Appendix.)

Caliber effectiveness

What Ellifritz found is that the major defensive pistol calibers – 9mm, .40S&W, and .45ACP – had terminal results that were very similar to each other. Any difference, he discovered, was well within the margin of error expected of the data. They all required an average of just over two rounds to achieve incapacitation; they all had a 50% chance (within a couple of percent) of actually incapacitating someone with a single shot; and, importantly, when they completely failed to incapacitate regardless of the number of shots fired, they all did so between 13% and 14% of the time. The results were so similar as to be slightly eery.

The most popular self defense rounds are the .45ACP, .40 S&W, 9mm Luger (Parabellum), and .380ACP. Is one better than the other?

Even the lowly .380ACP cartridge, derided by many in the gun world as "ineffective," actually did pretty well in the results he tabulated. Calibers below that did very poorly, but larger calibers didn't do all that much better. When we get to the 9mm, the calibers above don't do any statistically better job.

What can we determine from looking at his data closely? It appears that there is a lower limit of effectiveness, a "floor," at roughly the .380ACP level; below that point effectiveness drops off rapidly, and above that point doesn't increase dramatically. (It would probably be more precise to say that the .380ACP is like the basement, while the 9mm, .40 S&W, and .45ACP all occupy the main floor. There is no second story.)

While there are some who will maintain that the larger calibers, such as the .40S&W and the .45ACP, are more effective, the hard data to prove that supposition doesn't exist (to the best of my knowledge). The data seem to show that the difference between the common self-defense calibers is so small as to be inconsequential.

When picking a self-defense cartridge there are other factors to consider, however.

Recoil and controllability

The thing that strikes me about Ellifritz's data is how often (about half of the time) it takes more than one shot to incapacitate an attacker. In other words, you are likely to need to fire multiple times in order to get your attacker to stop whatever it was that made you shoot in the first place.

This is why the training world has long since gone to a model of "shoot until the threat stops." In the old days of defensive shooting training, people were often taught to shoot once or twice then lower the gun to see if their shots had the desired effect. Today we understand that process just gives the bad guy more time to attack. That's why virtually everyone, from military to law enforcement to the private sector, now teaches students to continue to shoot until the attacker no longer presents a threat. The goal in defensive shooting is to stop the threat, and we shoot however many rounds are needed to do that job.

This is why I tell my students that their task is to deliver rapid, multiple, accurate hits on target. They need to train to deliver whatever number of rounds it takes in the shortest time possible to the level of precision necessary (more on that concept later). That means that they need to control their guns in realistic strings of fire: three, four, perhaps even five (or more) rounds in very rapid succession.

The more the gun recoils, the more difficult that job will be. A caliber that produces more recoil will take longer (and require more control) to come back on target and be ready for the next shot. It's simple physics, really; no matter how good the shooter, he or she will take more time to deliver shots to a given level of precision with a heavier-recoiling pistol than one that doesn't recoil as much. That means one of two things: either the shooter will take more time to get equivalent hits, or take the same amount of time and score inaccurate rounds on target. The latter is unacceptable, so most people default to the former: they shoot slower with heavier calibers.

As we learned earlier, the effectiveness of all of the major self-defense calibers is roughly the same (well within the margin of error of the study). The choice, then, really comes down to shooting a certain number bullets in a specific amount of time with a larger, heavier-recoiling caliber or shooting

You need to be able to control your gun in realistic strings of fire – rapid, multiple, accurate rounds on target.

more rounds of equivalent effect in the same amount of time. I don't know about you, but for me more bullets of equivalent effect beats less bullets when it comes time to defend my life.

If you can deliver three or perhaps four rounds with a lighter-recoiling cartridge in the same time you'd shoot two rounds from the bigger caliber, that's less time the bad guy is going to get to hurt you. Remember: more bullets of equivalent effectiveness beats less bullets delivered in any given amount of time.

Which caliber do I recommend you choose?

That choice between controllability and effectiveness is why I recommend the 9mm round for the vast majority of defensive shooters. With modern hollowpoint ammunition it gives up nothing in terminal effect, but its milder recoil means that it can be fired to any given level of precision faster than a larger caliber.

Yes, some people can shoot the heavier calibers extremely well. There are lots of people who can shoot a .45ACP better than I can shoot a 9mm, but that's not really important. What is important is that no matter how well someone shoots a .40S&W or a .45ACP, he or she will shoot a 9mm better. The person who can beat me shooting a .45ACP will run rings around me when handed a softer-recoiling 9mm.

That's not the only advantage, though. The 9mm pistols hold more rounds in any given gun size than will a .40S&W or .45ACP. A subcompact 9mm will still carry 10 rounds, while the equivalent gun in .45ACP will only carry

Subcompact guns compared – 9mm Glock carries 10+1 rounds, while small 1911-style .45 only has 6+1.

seven or eight. (Another benefit: those ultra-small guns often have brutal recoil, and the reduced recoil of the 9mm makes them far more shootable than the other calibers.)

While no ammunition is cheap these days, 9mm ammo is usually less expensive than its larger brothers. Training to a high level of proficiency will cost less with the 9mm than any other caliber, which is never an unimportant consideration.

Are there times when the .380ACP is a valid choice?

The .380ACP is a much-maligned cartridge among the "experts" in the self defense world. It's derided as being a "mousegun" round (a small bullet capable of only killing a mouse, and only then at close range), but the general public buys guns chambered for the .380 in huge numbers. There seems to be a disconnect: people in the industry say it's only good for plinking tin cans, yet it's been a perennial good seller for decades. Who's right?

As I mentioned earlier, Ellifritz's data show that the .380ACP isn't quite as effective as any of the larger calibers – yet it's far more effective than any of the smaller cartridges. Even when compared to the most often-recommended defensive calibers it still looks pretty good; far more than its "mousegun" appellation would have you believe. Still, we have to acknowledge two things: first, that it will (on average) take more shots to incapacitate a potential attacker, and that it will fail to incapacitate a little more often than the "big boys."

Given that verifiable drop in performance, is there a reason to pick the .380ACP in preference to something else? Actually, there may be.

There are at least two occasions when I'll suggest to someone that they might consider the .380. First, someone who is very sensitive to recoil may pick the round because it's less painful to shoot. I've told this story countless times, but I know a lady who carries a Browning BDA pistol – a relatively large, heavy gun that carries twelve .380ACP cartridges in its double-stack magazine. It's larger and heavier than many compact 9mm pistols (and by compact I don't mean the really small ones).

I tried to convince her to ditch that big thing with the mousegun round (yes, I was one of "those" people back then) and pick up a similarly-sized 9mm. Luckily for her she knew her own mind and limitations; she had a condition which made physical control of a pistol very difficult and painful. She found that she couldn't handle the sharp recoil of the 9mm, but could shoot the .380 very quickly (and accurately). She reasoned – and this is going to sound very familiar – that four or six rounds of .380, delivered rapidly, would beat perhaps two rounds of 9mm delivered much more slowly. She was right, and she practiced to do exactly that. I'm glad I was unable to change her mind, because my caliber zeal caused me to be in the wrong.

Rapid, multiple, accurate hits on target. That's the goal.

The other instance where I'll recommend a preference for the .380ACP is when someone needs an exceptionally small gun. There are 9mm subcompacts made today that are the same size (in some cases markedly smaller)

Putting a 9mm cartridge in a gun nearly as small as a .380ACP model can result in control issues for some shooters.

than a lot of .380 pistols, and they're huge sellers. People buy them because they're small, light, and incredibly easy to hide in even the most restrictive wardrobe. The problem is that they're incredibly difficult to shoot well in anything resembling a realistic string of defensive fire.

I was given the opportunity, along with several other shooting instructors, to shoot one such gun. It had been recently introduced and was extremely difficult to get because its very compact size had made it very popular. I picked it up and fired a realistic string of defensive fire, meaning that I shot it at the same rate of speed with which I shoot most other guns. My hits were all over the place, and two hit clear out on the edges of the full-sized target we were using. The gun simply recoiled so viciously and twisted in my hands so severely that it was simply uncontrollable. (It's not as though I'm unaccustomed to recoil, either; I routinely shoot heavy calibers that most people find very painful to handle. I had it gripped as hard as I could, and still couldn't control it at that rate of fire.)

Only by slowing way down was I able to get accurate hits with the thing. At the pace I shot I could have placed perhaps double the number of .380 rounds in the same space of time. Now remember that I'm an experienced shooter, and then think about what happens when the average (non-experienced) person buys one of those guns.

If someone really needs a super-compact gun but isn't well trained and experienced, I'll sometimes recommend that they consider a similarly-sized

.380 instead. (Frankly, if I were given the choice between that subcompact 9mm I shot and the same gun in .380, I'd likely pick the latter.)

"Pick the biggest caliber you can shoot accurately"

You'll hear this advice very frequently, both in gun stores an in the online forums. It sounds quite profound and practical, but in reality it doesn't stand up to scrutiny.

Just about anyone can shoot just about any caliber accurately – for one round. It's easy to get a solid hit to any given level of precision when you don't have to worry about an immediate follow-up shot. All you need to do is hold the gun on target until the bullet has left the barrel.

If you leave enough space between that first shot and any subsequent shot, then it's like firing a single all over again. Shoot slowly enough, and you'll find that you're "accurate" (more on this in a later chapter) with just about anything.

It's only when you start to shoot more rapidly, one shot after another, that the recoil of the specific cartridge starts to affect your ability to hit the target. Now you have to deal with recoil control to set yourself up for the next shot; you have to re-align the gun on target quickly; and the effects of recoil on your body start to be felt, driving you backward and causing discomfort. All of that will affect where each of your subsequent shots hit.

So, the adage should really be "pick the biggest caliber you can shoot quickly." Now we have another problem: what's "quickly"? Since larger calibers generate more recoil, they will slow you down if you want to deliver rounds to any given level of precision. So now you have to decide how much deviation in your shots you'll accept to shoot at a certain speed. How do you make the tradeoff, particularly when you've learned (through Ellifritz's data) that the effect of the bullets is going to be pretty close to equal?

Finally, over how many rounds will you make your decision? It's relatively easy to fire two extremely rapid shots, even with a heavy recoiling gun, into a small area. Add a third shot at that same pace and the size of the group will widen considerably; a fourth will usually expand it drastically. It's easy to find defensive shootings where that many (or more) rounds were needed to stop the threat; so what's the definition of "quickly"?

This is why the adage makes no sense and provides no help to selecting a self-defense caliber. What should you be looking for instead? An effective caliber that you shoot the fastest into any given size of target, regardless of the number of rounds.

No matter who you are, you'll more than likely shoot a 9mm faster under those conditions. Again: more bullets of equal effect into a given area very quickly is a better prescription for success than fewer of those bullets in the same amount of time (or, worse, a longer amount of time).

Rapid, multiple, accurate hits on target. That's the goal. In a later chapter we'll talk about what accuracy is, and isn't.

---

[6] http://www.activeresponsetraining.net

[7] http://www.activeresponsetraining.net/an-alternate-look-at-handgun-stopping-power

CHAPTER 4

AMMUNITION
FOR DEFENSIVE
SHOOTING

What is your goal when you fire your pistol in a defensive encounter? Simple, really: it's to make the bad guy stop whatever it is that required you to shoot in the first place. You want to stop the threat; while doing so may result in your attacker's death, that's not the reason you shoot. Your focus must always remain on causing your attacker to stop hurting you, and the only way to do that is to do sufficient physical damage that he's forced to break off his attack.

MECHANISMS OF STOPPING THE THREAT

A "stop," that is a cessation of an attack through the attacker's incapacitation, can be due to either of two mechanism: psychological, where the attacker makes the decision that he really doesn't want to persist any longer; and physiological, where the attacker's body involuntarily stops functioning because of the damage that has been inflicted upon it. Both happen in defensive shootings.

Psychological stops

Psychological incapacitation is very unpredictable. There are people who will stop and run when confronted by a well-thrown rock, while others will remain undeterred by Mace, Tasers, and baton hits without so much as flinching. This is particularly true with people who are drunk or on drugs; their sensation of pain is dulled, and very often their intoxication results in antagonistic or psychotic behavior that is very resistant to psychological trauma.

9mm 115 grain round on left is light & fast – about 1300 feet per second. 230 grain .45 ACP round is heavy & slow, clocking in around 900 fps. Both have good track records – but why?

Since psychological stops are all in the mind and people's minds vary significantly (especially when intoxicated or otherwise under the influence), you simply can't count on delivering a jolt to a criminal's psyche reliably enough to cause him (or her) to stop in all cases. Instead, you'll need to focus on doing enough physical damage to your attacker to make it impossible for him to continue to function.

Physiological stops

As it happens, a bullet needs to do two things in order to deliver a level of physical impairment that will result in an involuntary shut down:

1) It has to get to something the body finds immediately important, and

2) It has to do rapid and significant disruption to that thing when it arrives.

Either, by itself, simply won't reliably cause the physical damage necessary for incapacitation. If the round fails at either of these tasks, any incapacitation that occurs is probably psychological in nature – which I hope you now understand is both unpredictable and unreliable.

The better the bullet performs those tasks, the faster incapacitation is likely to occur. Note that I said "likely." Handgun rounds are underpowered things and the human body is incredibly resilient; that combination means that nothing is ever certain. Your goal should be to stack the deck in your favor by eliminating as many variables as possible.

Yes, small caliber bullets fail. Guess what?
Large caliber bullets fail, too.

While this may sound like heresy to some, the fact is that within certain limits it doesn't really matter what the caliber is or what the bullet is made of or how fast it travels, as long as it does both of those tasks noted above. That's why there seems to be such a wide range of calibers, weights and velocities that work in defensive shootings; there is a pretty big envelope in terms of how that job can be done, and that envelope contains quite a number of cartridges and bullets.

The reason that the "heavy and slow" and "light and fast" apologists exist is because, generally, both choices just happen do both of the tasks on a fairly regular basis. Arguing about which is the better approach is really quite silly, because when they work it's because they did both tasks. When they fail, it's because they didn't do one (or both) of the tasks.

Here's the reality: yes, small caliber bullets fail. Guess what? Large caliber bullets fail, too. A good friend gave me a first-person account of a battle incident wherein a fellow soldier absorbed several solid torso hits and was still able to jump from his vehicle and get to the side of a country road before finally collapsing. The gun in question? A .50 caliber heavy machine gun. Yes, you read that correctly. Nothing – absolutely nothing – works every single time.

You must understand that when it comes to firearms and the human body, everything and anything can fail. Your job is to choose a caliber and bullet that seem to do those two tasks fairly reliably, and understand that there may be times that it just isn't enough. That's why you train and practice.

GETTING TO SOMETHING IMPORTANT

No matter what bullet is used, the person shooting that bullet needs to be capable of putting it on a course that will lead it to something important. Some cartridges are simply more challenging to shoot, particularly so when firing the rapid, multiple shots that are a necessity in defensive shooting. The first bullet needs to get to something the attacker's body finds immediately important – but so do the second and third and fourth. A cartridge that you can't control in realistic strings of fire is going to be less effective than one that you can.

Once the bullet is fired it has to defeat some obstacles to reach something important. Those obstacles include clothing, skin (which is a lot tougher than you might believe), bone and muscle. It has to penetrate all of those.

Penetration is key

When dealing with conventional solid bullets, the caliber (diameter), weight, and shape of the bullet all affect the penetration. All other things being equal, the more pointed the bullet the more it will penetrate; heavier bullets usually result in more penetration as well.

Expanding bullets (softnose or hollowpoint) increase their diameter when they enter the target. The frontal area increases dramatically as the bullet expands and acts something like a parachute, slowing the bullet and reducing penetration. This can be a problem if the penetration is reduced to the point that the bullet fails to have sufficient penetration, so expansion needs to be carefully controlled in order to be useful.

Too much penetration can be as bad as too little. A bullet with excessive penetration can move through the target and endanger innocents behind. This isn't a theoretical issue; there are records of police shootings where people have been hit and killed by bullets that had already penetrated the body of someone else.[8] It's important from both a performance and a safety standpoint to have a bullet that has sufficient penetration, but not an excessive amount.

Some cartridges will travel through multiple targets when loaded with streamlined, roundnosed bullets, but when loaded with expanding bullets will stop inside the first one. As it turns out, this has major benefits to the second task.

DOING WORK WHEN IT GETS THERE

I often refer to the second task as "doing work," because that's exactly what the bullet does. Its work just happens to be doing damage to the target.

The only reason a bullet does anything at all is because of its kinetic (moving) energy, and once it reaches its target the energy in a bullet can only do one of two things: it can be used to inflict damage to the target (work), or it can be wasted beyond the target.

As the bullet travels through the target, it uses its energy to crush or displace the clothing, skin, bone, muscle or organs it encounters. The amount of energy used is highly dependent on its shape: the more streamlined the bullet, the less work it does and the less energy it uses. If the bullet has a flattened shape it needs more energy to get through the target than it does if it has a nice, smooth, round nose.

If the bullet expands in the target, some of its energy is used to deform the bullet itself and the rest is used to push the much larger, flatter profile through the target. In some cases it uses up all its energy trying to get through the target and never makes it out the other side. This is how, as alluded to above, penetration can be controlled through the use of an expanding bullet.

The advantage of the expanding hollowpoint

The second task is that, once the bullet gets to something the body deems immediately important, it does rapid and significant disruption. This is where the expanding bullet, most commonly the hollowpoint, has a significant advantage: once expanded it presents a much larger frontal area to impact whatever it contacts. That large expanded nose, many times larger in area than the diameter of the bullet, does a lot more disruption than its non-expanding counterparts. Expanding bullets are therefore more effective and far more desirable.

Since the energy to deform the bullet is supplied by the bullet's movement, there needs to be enough remaining energy after expansion to do the necessary work. This is why I say that the bullet has to do rapid and significant disruption when it arrives; if it gets there but has so little energy left that it is incapable of inflicting necessary damage, then it is nearly as if it had not gotten there to begin with.

Don't misunderstand: I'm not saying that the bullet's wound in such a case isn't serious! It is, but our goal in a defensive shooting is to make the attacker stop what he's doing by compromising his ability to function – and the sooner that happens the better. The only reliable way to make him do that is to disrupt an important physiological function. If that doesn't happen quickly, it's possible that the defender – that would be you – could be injured or even killed while we're waiting for the attacker to pass out.

The classic example is a criminal who gets shot with a lowly .22 rimfire. He will likely still be able to complete his assault even though he might succumb to peritonitis a few days later. That wound certainly isn't trivial, but since it didn't achieve the goal of stopping the criminal before he could harm someone else it has failed. Your overriding goal, remember, is to stop the bad guy.

CHOOSING DEFENSIVE AMMUNITION

Many years of shooting data has shown that the best defensive ammunition is a hollowpoint bullet that expands reliably in the target and penetrates sufficiently to reach vital organs. There may be instances where that choice isn't possible, but for the vast majority of people under the vast majority of circumstances the modern bonded hollowpoint is what's needed.

In 9mm, best results seem to come from the mid- to heavy-weight bullets (124 grains to 147 grains), usually in +P loadings. I'm a fan of Speer's Gold Dot 124 grain +P and Winchester's PDX1 124 grain +P, both of which have excellent reputations. The Speer in particular is in wide police service and has a very good track record.

If you're using a .40 S&W, I would suggest the 165 grain loads from Speer (Gold Dot) and Winchester. For those who insist on carrying a .45 ACP, any of the 230 grain modern (bonded) hollowpoints from Speer, Winchester, Federal, or Remington will most likely be fine.

What about +P ammo?

Remember that hollowpoints use part of their energy to expand their diam-

+P ammunition is loaded to higher pressures and achieves greater velocity, which may result in greater penetration and expansion.

eter, but the energy that's used to expand the bullet is energy that can't used to drive the same bullet forward. There is no such thing as a free lunch; if you want the bullet to expand, it's going to use energy. If there is too little of it to start with, there won't be enough left to carry the bullet on its path.

In those cases the expanded bullet will stop forward movement too soon, resulting in very shallow wounds that don't reach vital organs. (This is why you don't find a lot of expanding bullets in generally slow calibers, like the old .38 Special – there just isn't enough energy to drive a bullet deeply into the target and expand it at the same time.)

The answer is to start out with more energy, enough to both expand the bullet and penetrate sufficiently. This is often accomplished with "+P" ammunition, which is simply a cartridge that has been loaded beyond what is considered "normal" pressure. The +P loading boosts the energy of the cartridge to accomplish a specific task.

A common misunderstanding of +P loadings is that since they're not a huge increase in power they're useless. Here's the thing: they don't have to be.

The idea behind the +P is to add enough energy to reliably deliver an expanded bullet deep enough to do its job. It doesn't have to be a lot of extra energy – it just has to be enough. If a normal-pressure load can't quite deliver that bullet to where it needs to, but a little hotter +P version does, then that is sufficient for the task at hand.

It's important to understand that you don't need vast increases in power for defensive applications; you simply need enough power to perform both of the tasks we discussed earlier. Some will argue that it's better to have a larger reserve amount of energy on tap than a +P, but everything comes at a price. In the chapters on technique we'll delve into that a little more.

---

[8]Ayoob, Massad F.: "The Gun Digest Book of Concealed Carry", ISBN 9780896896116

CHAPTER 5

TESTING YOUR PISTOL FOR RELIABILITY

The most important functional characteristic of a defensive pistol is reliability. If the pistol isn't reliable, if it jams or otherwise malfunctions when you need it most, it has failed at its primary task and isn't just useless – it's actually dangerous.

It's important, then, that any gun that is new to you, regardless of its source or age, be tested to make sure that it is capable of functioning as it should when you really need it.

WHAT WE'RE TESTING

When we test a pistol for defensive reliability, we're looking at two separate (but very much interrelated) things.

First, does the pistol simply function as expected, as the manufacture intended? Does it load, fire, extract, eject, reload, and lock the slide open when it's empty? Second, does it do all of those things correctly with the specific ammo you plan to carry in it?

They would seem to be the same thing, but they're really not. In the first case, we test simply to make sure that there are no flaws in our particular gun that would render it non-functional regardless of the ammunition being used. For instance, does the trigger actually work? Do any safeties function as intended? Do the magazines seat and lock in properly? Is there an extrac-

tor in place? Is the firing pin (or striker) broken? If it has a hammer, does it "follow" the slide and cause the gun to go "full auto"? Do the magazines feed properly?

All of those things relate to whether the gun is serviceable, but don't really touch on whether it's serviceable for us, in our particular use. It's the second test where we check for compatibility – the gun and our chosen ammunition get along together – and that the ammunition shoots properly to point-of-aim (meaning that the bullets hit where the sights are aligned).

Why separate them? Primarily because of the cost. Good defensive ammunition these days is quite expensive, and using that ammo for testing that is just as easily done with cheaper ball or FMJ rounds is a drain on the pocketbook for very little gain.

Test the gun for overall function with cheap target ammunition, and only then check it for compatibility with your favorite defense load.

If you've got a gun in which you already have confidence, but wish to change the type or brand of defensive ammunition you carry, you can skip the first test phase completely. You already know the gun works, the only question is will it work with the new ammunition?

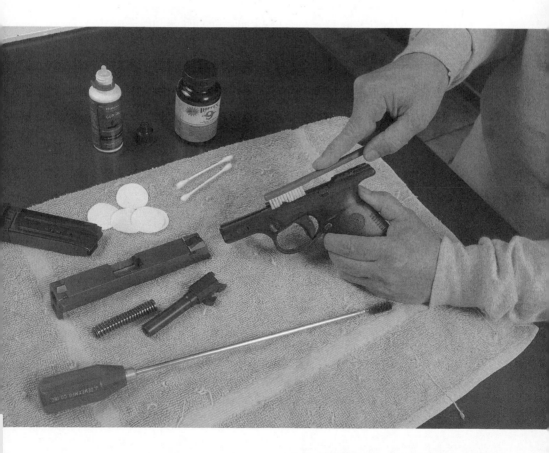

HOW TO TEST YOUR DEFENSIVE PISTOL

For Phase One, you'll need your pistol, all of the magazines you have, and a couple of boxes (100 rounds) of good quality target ammunition from a major manufacturer.

First things first

Clean and lubricate the gun according to the manufacturer's specifications. Yes, even if it's new. Many pistols have only minimal lubrication from the factory, and if the gun has been sitting on a shelf for more than a month or so it's likely that the lubes used are now oxidized. Cleaning and lubing the gun prior to testing puts it into a known baseline condition from which you can make proper judgments.

If the gun is new to you, whether brand new or pre-owned, the gun needs to pass a fundamental safety check. Load a magazine with two rounds (and only two). Chamber the first round and fire; check to see that the slide is still forward, in battery, indicating that it's ready to fire the second round. Press the trigger again to fire the second round, and then check to make sure that the slide is locked back. If it's not, drop the magazine and lock the slide open.

If it can't fire 100 rounds of the best possible ammunition, it's not reliable for personal defense.

What this test does is to make sure that the mechanism of the pistol does not fire more than one round with each press of the trigger. If after you fire the first round the slide is locked back and the magazine is empty, that would mean that the gun had "doubled" – fired both rounds with one pull of the trigger. That's an unsafe condition, and one that makes the gun technically an illegal machine pistol. If the slide wasn't locked back but the second trigger press resulted only in a "click" and the magazine was empty, that too would indicate a dangerous doubling condition.

Expanding bullet uses part of its available energy in mushrooming. Careful ammunition choice ensures that there's enough energy left for proper penetration. (Photo courtesy of Hornady Manufacturing.)

To pass this test, the gun must fire each round with a separate press of the trigger. If it doesn't, the gun needs to be repaired immediately.

Phase One

If the pistol passed (or it's not a gun which is new to you), go ahead and load all of your magazines; if you have so many magazines that you can't load all of them with the 100 rounds, split the ammo evenly among them.

Fire the first magazine at a slow pace, making sure that all of the pistol's functions work. At the last shot the slide should lock open; if it doesn't, set that magazine aside (failure to lock open is usually a magazine issue, but if it happens repeatedly with other magazines there's likely a gun problem).

Drop the magazine, insert the next one, and fire all the rounds at a more rapid rate. Repeat with each of the remaining magazines; if you need to refill the magazines to shoot all of the ammunition, do so. By the end of the 100 rounds you should be able to tell if the gun is reliable.

What's the standard? Zero malfunctions of any type (other than those that are positively traceable to a specific magazine). If the pistol can't pass this simple test it's unreliable for defensive use. It doesn't matter how much you like it or if it's a good brand name or how expensive it is, if it can't fire 100 rounds of the best possible ammunition, it's not reliable for personal defense. Get it fixed or get rid of it.

Phase Two

If (and only if) the gun passed the preliminary check and Phase One, you'll need 50 rounds of you chosen defensive ammunition. This time load your magazines to capacity (if you identified a faulty magazine in Phase One, don't use it for this test).

Fire the first magazine slowly, checking for both function (feeding and ejecting) and that the impact of the rounds agrees with your sights. Shoot carefully to determine if the sights and that ammunition both agree: the bullets need to hit where the sights are aimed. If not, adjust the sights; if the sights aren't adjustable, make a note of how far off the hits are, in what direction, and at what range.

Shoot the remaining rounds in rapid fire. Very often you'll find a pistol that functions perfectly when shot slowly and deliberately, but chokes when shot rapidly (as you're likely to do when faced with a lethal threat).

Again, the standard is zero malfunctions, of any type, in 50 rounds.

What if the ammunition doesn't hit to point of aim?

If the bullets aren't hitting where your sights are aimed and you don't have adjustable sights, you have a decision to make. If the gun is otherwise functional with that ammo, it's worth visiting a knowledgeable gunsmith who might be able to find replacement sights that will bring the bullet holes into alignment. If not, he might be able to modify the ones you have to do so.

If neither of those proves to be an option, you can either change your ammunition (and re-test), or change the gun (and re-test). One thing that's not an option: carrying a gun that delivers bullets to a different place than you intend.

How much variation is acceptable? I'd say no more than an inch or so at a

It's critical that your bullets go where you intend them to go; if your shots are this far off your point of aim, you need to fix the problem before carrying that gun/ammo combination.

common, plausible shooting distance (say, across your bedroom or the length of your car).

TRAINING AS RELIABILITY TESTING?

A good defensive shooting course can be a way to test the true reliability of your pistol. In fact, I generally won't carry a pistol that I haven't trained with, for two reasons: first, it tells me whether or not the gun is functionally reliable, that it will work even under somewhat trying circumstances; second, it identifies problems with my relationship to the pistol – such as minor fit problems, comfort concerns, and my ability to operate the controls efficiently.

What constitutes a "good" course from the standpoint of reliability? I'd say any course that requires you to shoot around 500 rounds per day; a two-day course of 1,000 rounds is even better!

But I'm unlikely to ever shoot more than 12 rounds, total!

Yes, that's true. There are people who believe that because their pistol will, at most, ever be expected to fire two full magazines, that many rounds is sufficient testing.

The reality is that you may only fire a magazine (or perhaps two) when it counts, but what will your gun's condition be when it's called upon to do so? A freshly cleaned gun is one thing, but one which has been carried in a holster (particularly in a dirty environment, like a pocket) will collect lint and dust and all kinds of debris that can affect its functioning. The lubricants, too, will deteriorate fairly quickly, especially when exposed to heat or humidity. Oil can migrate off of the surfaces it's supposed to lubricate, leaving them with more friction than when everything was fresh. All of this affects the gun's function, and sometimes dramatically so. Add in the effects of cold or wet, and the pistol that's perfectly reliable for a couple of magazines right after a thorough cleaning might not make it through a single one.

Ideally we'd clean our guns and then artificially age them so that we could test what happens when dirt and lack of lubrication combine, but that would be difficult for most people to do. A high-round-count training course, however, is a good substitute.

If it doesn't make the grade, set it aside (or sell it) and buy something more reliable. Your life is worth it!

After shooting 500 or 1,000 rounds your gun will be dirty and the oils will have slung off; it may even have collected some native soil or, better yet, perhaps a little rain. All of these things serve to put it closer to a gun that's been carried in its holster for a month or so than just about anything else you could do. Think of a training course as artificially aging your gun in a way that also gives you the benefit of increased skill and confidence, in a controlled environment where you can identify and fix the problems that crop up.

If your gun makes it through such a course without malfunction, you can be sure that it will hold up no matter what the environmental conditions are when you're attacked and need it to perform.

What to look for

Your gun should be able to make it through at least 500 rounds (and preferably 1,000) without any malfunction that is not positively identified as being from defective ammunition. My personal opinion is that if your pistol can't feed at least 500 rounds of new FMJ ammunition from a major manufacturer, in one day without any supplemental oiling or cleaning, it simply isn't reliable enough for personal defense.

This means 500 rounds with zero malfunctions: no failures to feed, fire, extract, or eject, and of course no parts breakage. The harsh reality I've observed (over many classes I've taken and taught) is that not all pistols can do so. The even harsher reality is that some guns have proven to me that they are simply more reliable than others (just as some automobiles are more reliable than others).

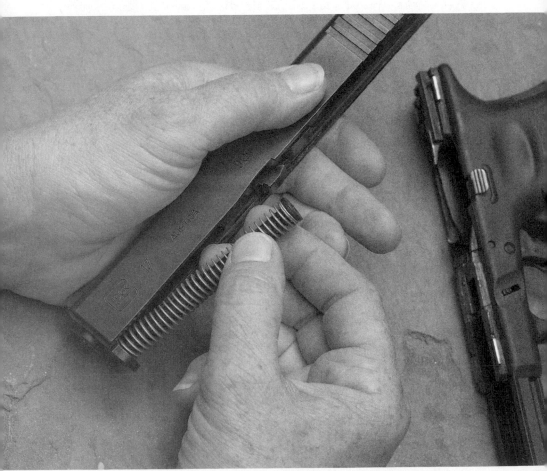

Changing the recoil spring is recommended by all pistol manufacturers; it not only solves function problems, but prolongs the life of the pistol.

Changing the magazine springs ensures proper feeding.

Take your gun through a solid training course, shoot at least 500 rounds in one day during that course and be honest with yourself: if it didn't make the grade, set it aside (or sell it) and buy something more reliable. Your life is worth it!

SOME THOUGHTS ON USED SEMI-AUTOMATIC PISTOLS

Lots of people (including yours truly) buy used pistols for self defense. Sometimes it's to save money, while other times it's to get a particularly desirable gun that isn't available new, but whatever the reason it's important to do some maintenance to the gun before testing it and relying on it for protection.

Whenever I buy a used pistol I immediately replace the recoil spring. It's a normal wear part, and most manufacturers will tell you to replace it (depending on the maker, of course) anywhere from every 500 to every 2,000 rounds. A weak recoil spring will cause all kinds of malfunctions, and since they're so cheap and easy to replace it makes little sense not to.

If the pistol is more than ten years old, I'll also replace all of the magazine springs. They're more difficult to replace, but you'll find a lot of feed errors can be traced back to weak magazine springs. Again, they're cheap (much less than the cost of a new magazine) and a quick way to ensure that the gun operates correctly.

CHAPTER 6

REALITIES OF DEFENSIVE SHOOTING: THE AMBUSH ATTACK

I remember back when I first entered the defensive shooting world. I'd taken a few classes, read many of the classic books that everyone recommended (and often still recommend even though they're horribly outdated), and even shot some 'combat' matches now and again (because everyone said that they were a great way to practice "realistically"). I thought I had a good idea of what would happen if I ever needed to use my lawfully carried gun in self defense.

Then YouTube came along.

YouTube, along with the other video sharing sites on the internet, started showing dashcam and surveillance camera videos from all over the world. What they showed was something of a revelation to me; self defense incidents weren't like what I'd been taught or envisioned. They were fast, violent, nasty affairs wherein the criminal didn't politely stand at twenty-one feet, graciously show his knife, then start running at his victim. Instead he'd wait until he was within just a few feet and then suddenly – and without much, if any, warning – attack.

That was my wake-up call.

The ugly, gritty world of predatory attacks bears little resemblance to this Hollywood-inspired encounter.

BOY, WAS I MISINFORMED!

Even though I consider myself immune to fiction, Hollywood depictions of violence were a lot closer to what I'd imagined would happen than were these new, gritty videos. But as I watched video after video of people getting severely beaten – or even killed – I slowly learned that very often, the reality of a criminal attack isn't like what we're shown in the movies or on television. What's worse is that they don't often have much resemblance to what many shooting instructors teach. That's because the criminal attack usually happens faster, and with far less warning, than anyone really expects.

After that, I confess I went through several years of being afraid that I wouldn't be able to defend myself with the gun that was on my hip every day. Though I told myself my training was the best available and that my diligent practice reinforced my above average skills (hey, I was even winning matches now and again!), somewhere deep in my mind I knew that being good at the wrong things wasn't being prepared.

I recommitted myself to training in ways that were congruent with what I was learning about real criminal attacks. The result is what you're now reading.

EVIDENCE-BASED TRAINING

In the old days of self-defense education (a mere thirty or forty years ago), the only basis for training in defensive shooting were the stories that people who had "been there" were willing to tell. Today we know that first-person accounts of traumatic events are rarely accurate,[9,10] but back then we didn't. We took them at face value, and so much of the defensive shooting doctrine from that era is based on participant's flawed, subjective recollections. Much of that doctrine still persists in some quarters.

Fights are polite in comparison to the way a predator extracts what he wants from his victim.

As time went by, technology and science came to our rescue. Technology in the form of ubiquitous video, like the police cruiser dashcams and video surveillance, made sure that more crimes were caught from an objective viewpoint. The internet played a role as well, because much of that footage ends up online where it can be seen by anyone. Today any interested student of self defense can do a quick search and find hours of real-life video showing what happens when people are forced to defend themselves. What's scary to the uninitiated is that most of those videos show not fights, but attacks: vicious, brutal, and targeted attacks. Fights are polite in comparison to the way a predator extracts what he wants from his victim.

At the same time, we've learned a tremendous amount about how the body reacts to a lethal threat. The National Institutes of Health (NIH) says that we've learned more about the brain in the last ten years than we knew in all of recorded history up to that point.[11] This new knowledge includes revelations about how our brains make decisions in critical situations, how it processes information, and what it directs the rest of the body to do when faced with a lethal threat. Because of this incredible progress in science, we now know that there are specific natural reactions to a lethal threat, reactions that can't be trained away or ignored.[12]

Any training program on which you embark must be evidence-based if you expect that training to hold up in the face of an actual attack. Evidence-based training must take into consideration the latest information, both what we know about how attacks happen and what we know about how the body reacts to those threats.

Ubiquitous security cameras preserve video of actual attacks for later analysis.

GENERALIZED AWARENESS ISN'T ENOUGH

One of the doctrines that came out of the early ages of defensive training was the idea that some level of generalized 'situational awareness' would keep you safe. There was a time when I too believed that, until I started to see the video evidence. It became clear that there was a serious flaw in that advice, a flaw of which even the least intellectually endowed criminal could take advantage.

The flaw is simple: you can't be completely aware of everything, every minute of the day, because you have a life to live. No matter how much attention you pay to your surroundings, sooner or later you're going to need to

No matter how aware you are, even if you're always "swiveling" your head, something can still catch your attention, giving a predator the opening for his attack.

read the menu or watch the movie or supervise your children or look into the eyes of your date. That's life, and those distractions happen hundreds of times a day to even the best of us. (Frankly, if they didn't I'm not sure I'd like my life all that much! Continual paranoia is not fun.)

This isn't to completely discount the value of being aware of your surroundings, only to put it in perspective. You can't be aware of everything around you all the time. You can be aware of some of the stuff all of the time, or all of the stuff some of the time, but not all of the stuff all of the time. At

Criminals often set up their own distractions, like asking for the time or directions, to get within striking distance.

some point you'll return to being human and pay attention to something else. That's just natural.

What's also natural is that this is the point at which you are most vulnerable and, not coincidentally, the point at which the savvy attacker will often choose to initiate contact. Superb situational awareness may only delay the inevitable; an attacker who is sufficiently motivated (i.e., there is something he really wants) to attack a person displaying good awareness may choose to bide his time, knowing that within a short period of time something will attract the victim's attention – then he can strike. That's why you still need self-defense skills, and more specifically self-defense skills that work when you're caught off-guard – when you've been ambushed.

Criminals often set up their own distractions. While the victim is busy dealing with an innocuous request or conversation ("hey buddy, you got the time?"), the attacker makes his move. Situational awareness can only go so far!

A training regimen that assumes you will always have advance notice of an attack due to superlative situational awareness is fundamentally flawed. It assumes a set of conditions that are probably unlikely to be continually present even with the most conscientious person, and which can often be manipulated to facilitate an attack.

AMBUSH: THE PREFERRED METHOD OF THE SAVVY CRIMINAL

Referring back to the work of Tom Givens, we find that his victims were almost always surprised by their attack. I refer to this as the criminal ambush: confronting someone suddenly and unexpectedly in order to commit a crime. Whether the criminal is physically concealed (waiting behind something) or psychologically concealed (obscured by social conditioning or distraction), he strikes when the victim does not know or expect that the attack is coming. The aim is to catch the victim off guard, and it usually works.

It's a little uncomfortable admitting that you can be surprised, but you can be. I can be. I've watched some ardent proponents of the situational awareness defense concept, and I've seen many times in their daily lives when they're distracted enough by things in their normal routine to be surprised. You need to come to grips with the idea that you may be starting "behind the eight-ball" against your attacker, and that your training must take that "worst case scenario" into account.

This understanding, this realization and admission, is vital. As I noted in the beginning, the ambush is the hardest attack from which to mount an effective defense. If you know ahead of time that you'll be attacked, you can be proactive: you can get into the perfect shooting stance and draw your gun to the perfect sight picture and use perfect trigger control to fire the perfect number of rounds into a perfect group, thus ending the fight. (Or, because you know it's coming, you could just run away before it happens!)

The skills required to mount a successful reactive, counter-ambush defense are very different than those used to initiate a proactive defense.

Think about all the times when you might be surprised – like taking care of your children's needs, for instance.

If you don't know the attack is coming until it happens, all of that goes out the window. Your body, conditioned by the inherited survival instincts of the millennia, behaves in a predictable manner that you've probably never before experienced. You don't get your perfect stance or perfect sight picture, and as a result of not training under such conditions you can't perfectly control your shots like you can on the shooting range. The result is an inefficient response that leaves you exposed to danger longer than is necessary.

The skills required to mount a successful reactive, counter-ambush defense are very different than those used to initiate a proactive defense. As I think you'll see in the coming chapters, what works for the proactive shooting probably doesn't work for the reactive defense. However, the reverse is different – because what works when you're in reactive mode still works when you do have a little preparation time.

Training for the ambush attack allows you to respond to the greatest range of plausible incidents and is therefore the most efficient way to train.

THE COUNTER-AMBUSH TRAINING MODEL

This is why your defensive shooting training regimen should be based on a counter-ambush training model: reacting to an attack that is surprising, chaotic, and threatening.

It's surprising, in the sense that you didn't know it was going to happen, largely because it happened when you were distracted by the normal happenings of everyday life. It's chaotic, in the sense that you don't know what's going to happen next and are forced into reacting to what's happening. It's threatening, in the sense that it poses an immediate and otherwise unavoidable danger to your life or limb – and it's a danger to which the correct response is shooting.

This is a specific kind of attack; it's not a fight, as I've said, because "fight" implies both consensual violence and a duration that's longer than the typical crime. What we're going to consider in these pages is the criminal ambush attack – a predatory attack – that's usually over a few seconds after you recognize that it's happening. It's a very small slice of time, but it's likely to be one of the longest six or eight seconds of your life!

Distance and the ambush

As I mentioned in the introduction, these attacks usually happen beyond two arm's reach but, as Tom Given's data shows us, usually within roughly 15 feet. If you think about it, that makes sense; the criminal attacker wants something from you, so he needs to get in fairly close proximity. (This, as opposed to the paid assassin who would simply shoot you from the shadows. Or blow up your car. Or poison your hamburger. You get the idea.)

Since criminals also often use distraction and misdirection to their advantage, they need to get within conversational distance to do so. This tends to explain the data that Givens has collected on those actual attacks his students faced.

The tower sniper or the mall terrorist or the active school shooter are the anomalies, the least likely of threats to face. That doesn't mean that you

Many attacks happen within conversational distance.

should completely ignore the possibility of facing one of them, only that you're much more likely to need to deal with the mugger coming around the back of your car and grabbing your door than the deranged killer with a rifle sniping at passers-by. The close-in ambush attack is, by the authoritative accounts I've found, the most common type of deadly force attack and is thus the most likely kind of incident you'll have to face. The rest of this book is devoted to helping you prepare for it.

[9]Pappas, Stephanie and Bryner, Jeanna: "Eyewitness Testimony Can Be Tragically Mistaken", http://www.livescience.com/16194-crime-eyewitnesses-mistakes.html

[10]Law, Bridget Murray: "Seared in our memories", Monitor On Psychology (American Psychological Association), September 2011, Vol 42, No. 8. http://www.apa.org/monitor/2011/09/memories.aspx

[11]Video transcript, "About the National Institute on Drug Abuse", National Institutes of Health. http://science.education.nih.gov/supplements/nih2/addiction/videos/about/transcript-about-nih.htm

[12]Taflinger, Richard F.: "Taking Advantage". Washington State University, http://public.wsu.edu/~taflinge/psych1.html

CHAPTER 7

YOUR BODY'S NATURAL REACTIONS

I f there is any such thing as a certainty in defensive shooting, it's the natural, instinctive reaction that occurs when you're surprised by a lethal threat. Instinctive reactions are those things that humans do without prior exposure or training; they are those things that are seemingly hard-wired in our brains from birth.[13] Reacting to a loud noise, for instance, is a readily observable trait in newborns; babies in the womb too are reported to react to a startling sound.

Instinctive reactions to threats have developed over millennia in the human animal; the ability to stay alive among predators, many of them easily able to take down homo sapiens, is why we're at the top of the food chain today. Without some sort of built-in mechanism to make our responses automatic (and without the necessity to think about them every time) we likely would not have made it this far because we would have needed to evaluate every single threat as a new experience every time; sooner or later, we'd lose.

It's important to understand that these natural reactions happen when you're truly surprised by an attack, and that they last for a relatively short period of time. The half-life of the catecholamine hormones that facilitate your reactions is measured in minutes,[14] which means that their effect starts deteriorating very rapidly after the onset of the reactions. Your body's reactions are therefore very short-duration events that, understood and prepared for in training, allow you to gain the upper hand when you're already behind the curve.

One of the salient points regarding your body's natural instinctive reactions is that they can't be trained away. You can learn to suppress their amplitude (through repeated exposure to a stimulus capable of initiating them) or to convert them to intuitive responses more efficiently, but they are almost certain to occur. Understanding them is the first step to taking advantage of them.

IDENTIFYING THE NATURAL REACTIONS

When faced with a lethal threat, your brain directs your body to make some rather amazing transformations.[15] There are many different reactions, some large and others almost unnoticeable, that enable you to deal with something that poses a threat to your existence. Detailing all of them would be a book in itself.

As it happens, it's not necessary for you to understand all of them. There are only about a half-dozen unique reactions[16] that are important from the standpoint of defensive shooting, important in the sense that they affect how and what you train. In the chapters that follow, you'll find techniques that build on and take advantage of these natural survival reactions, allowing you to respond more efficiently than forcing an unnatural, artificial technique into the situation (if you even could).

By training properly, you can make the transition from instinctive reaction to intuitive response faster, easier, and without cognitive thought.

External manifestations

Some of the body's natural reactions are external, meaning that they're observable. When you watch surveillance camera footage, you'll often see all three of these reactions, all happening approximately simultaneously or, at the very least, in extremely rapid succession. (The order in which I've presented them should not be taken as a timeline of any sort.)

Lowering center of gravity prepares the body to fight or run, as the situation dictates. Knees bend, body weight drops toward the ground.

• **Lowering of the body's center of gravity**

If you think about it, preparing for any physical activity – be it running away or fighting – requires that the body first drop its center of gravity. Stand in front of a mirror and try to move naturally without changing the height of your belly button; you'll find that you can do nothing more than a robot-like shuffling. When you need to move immediately, like when you're faced with a sudden threat, your body naturally drops its center of gravity to prepare for an extreme exertion. This puts your body in a superb position from which it can lunge or move rapidly to either side, both of which are definite survival positives when facing something that wants to eat you.

This lowering of the center of gravity looks like a shallow crouch; your knees bend causing your body to drop, while at the same time your upper torso leans forward at the hips to maintain balance; the buttocks are forced backward to compensate.

• Hands moving toward the line of sight

Humans, as you may have been told, are truly visual creatures. You derive a huge portion of what you know from what you see, and in a lethal encounter that's especially true: what you know of the threat comes mainly from what your eyes tell you. As a result, your mind is hard-wired to protect that most valuable asset.

When people are startled, their hands start to move in a protective manner toward their line of sight; they flinch toward the eyes. They don't always make it all the way, of course, for a number of reasons (including familiarity with certain stimuli). They do almost always at least start in that direction, however, and again you can see this very often in videos of actual surprise attacks.

When startled, one of the most common reactions is the movement of the hands toward the eyes, to protect the head.

One thing I've noticed is that this flinch, as we'll call it, is convulsive. The muscles that produce the movement tense suddenly and violently, throwing the hands into motion; the shoulders often hunch or roll forward in concert. Sometimes the flinch rises and subsides without the subject seemingly being aware that it even happened.

• Orienting to the threat

At the onset of a surprise stimulus, the body tends to orient, or position itself, toward whatever it is that is identified as being a potential threat. The head turns to put the threat into its line of sight, where binocular vision is at its most useful, and the body usually follows by squaring up to the threat so that it can employ its natural weapons – hands and feet.

The body's natural reactive position is facing the threat square on to get best visual information and to make the best use of defensive resources.

This is not a boxing stance, which is a learned position; the natural stance is neutral, in that the body is parallel to the threat and the feet are directly under the body, preparing to move in any direction needed. Any off-axis orientation, such as blading to the threat, would make movement to one side more difficult than the other; it should be easy to comprehend how that could be a detriment to survival.

Internal reactions

The external reactions are aided and supplemented by some internal reactions, all of which have to do with changes in blood flow in the body. The blood carries oxygen and the myriad of chemicals that serve to initiate all of the transformations that occur as a result of the threat.[17] As it happens, if you can see the external manifestations we just talked about, you know that these internal reactions have also occurred. The external reactions serve as markers that prove the internal ones are happening as well.

Again, in no particular order:

• Increase in resolution in the center of the field of vision

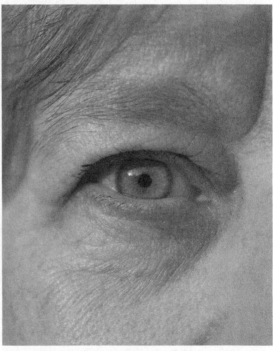

The retina of the eye uses rods and cones to collect and transmit image information to the optic nerve, and that information is sent to the visual cortex where it's interpreted as sight. In the middle of the retina is the fovea, which is populated exclusively by the cones (which have higher resolution and faster reaction times than the rods). As a result the fovea is capable of delivering a much higher level of detail than is the rest of the retina. When the body's alarm response is activated, changes in blood supply to the eye

Changes in blood flow to the eye affect focusing and increase resolution in the center of the field of vision.

cause most of the information to come from this center where all the cones are located. The result is an increase in resolution, though with a somewhat narrow angle of view relative to our normal sight. This has a very positive effect on survivability, because it allows the gathering of much more information specifically about the threat.

• **Reduction in blood flow to the extremities**

When faced with a sudden possibility of lethal injury, the body shunts blood from the extremities (hands and feet) to the larger muscle groups and the core. There are several explanations for this phenomenon, but the end result is a decrease in blood to the hands and fingers.

When blood flow is reduced there is a decrease in strength, dexterity, and tactile sensation. Hands might tremble a bit, have trouble doing complex tasks that rely on muscle control, and have less feeling. This sounds entirely negative, but consider the upside: that same reduced blood flow also means that damage to the extremities won't be felt as keenly, and injuries won't result in dangerous blood loss as quickly.

Those downsides, reduced dexterity and tactile sensation, are things that we have to work around when we design techniques for handling tools (the gun).

• **Distortions in the perception of time**

One of the more unusual natural reactions is a distortion in the perceived passage of time during a lethal attack. In most cases people report that time slows down, making things appear to be happening at a slower rate – including their own responses to what they're seeing. In reality both the person and the world are still moving at the same speed, but the brain reports that they're not.

This becomes a real issue if you have to do anything that requires visual input, since that's how the distortion occurs. Though you may believe you are moving slowly, in reality the rest of the world isn't – which means there is a disconnect between what you think is happening and what really is.

I've actually experienced this as the result of a severe fright. When I was in college I once parked on a seedy street in a not-terribly-good area of a large city. Walking back to my car I noticed a rather hulking male following me; I quickened my pace, but so did he. I ran to my car and tried to put my key into the door (this was long before the days of remote control locks). I clearly remember trying to get the key in the hole, knowing full well that there was someone closing in, but I couldn't seem to do it fast enough. I tried to speed up but that only caused me to fumble, which in turn fed my panic, which seemed to make things slow down even more! I finally got the key in the lock, jumped into the car and hit the lock button – about the time the fellow ran past me, yelling at a couple of other men on the far end of the block to "wait for me!"

There have been many explanations for why this phenomenon occurs,[18] and there is a lot of ongoing research to find out the exact neurological mechanism, but it's enough to understand that the effect occurs and that it affects both your emotional and physical reactions to what you're seeing.

Interestingly, some people report that time seems to speed up during an incident. Though research is still in its infancy, some of the most important researchers in the field of time distortions suggest[19] that it's a result of training or habituation to a stimulus. Those who have trained certain techniques or maneuvers to the point that they can do them without cognitive thought –

without being aware of directing themselves to do those things – are usually the ones who perceive that they're moving at a faster rate than they really are. This would appear to me to be a very real benefit of training.

In the chapters that follow I'll be referencing these natural reactions to explain why I recommend the things I do.

WORKING WITH THE BODY'S NATURAL REACTIONS

Why the focus on these reactions? As I said at the top, these reactions affect how and what we train. We go back to our task of efficiency, making the best use of our resources to achieve a specific goal: if the techniques you've trained run counter to what your body actually does when threatened, your response is likely to be delayed (or even circumvented). That's inefficient.

A more efficient response happens when you train techniques that work with the body's natural reactions. That's the basis of intuitive skills: things you learn that work well with the way your body works (as opposed to instinctive skills, which are generally considered to be "hard wired" into our brains and require no prior education or exposure).

What is intuitive?

You can learn to do a lot of things that aren't intuitive. Take, for instance, the horn in your car. The horn button is on the face of the steering wheel, usually in the middle or in a place where your open palm can mash it and get sound. In a panic situation your hands are already in proximity because they're

Hitting the horn in your car is an intuitive act because it works well with what your body does naturally.

on the wheel; all you have to do is flatten your palm and push forward, in the same direction your braking foot is already moving. It also keeps your hand in contact with the wheel, which is a big psychological advantage. Using the horn is a sympathetic movement that requires little to no training, because it works well with what your body is already doing (and prefers to do).

What if that horn button required you to reach to the side of the steering column and turn a little knob counter-clockwise? You could certainly learn to do so, but when that little kid darts out from between cars, oblivious to your presence, it wouldn't be an easy maneuver to perform. It doesn't work well with anything else your body is doing, and you might not end up doing it at all. It is non-intuitive.

It stands to reason that intuitive skills, those that work well with how the body already functions, are easier to learn, easier to remember, and more importantly easier to recall when needed because they are a more natural extension of the physical processes that you already do naturally. They are more efficient, and lead to a more efficient response.

Justifying non-intuitive skills?

As I said earlier, instinctive reactions cannot be trained away, because they're things that our bodies are hard-wired to do. You can decide to train in ways that work with those reactions or in ways that work against them, but in neither case can you replace them.

I've run into many people who insist on training in non-intuitive ways, ways that run counter to how science and medicine (and objective visual evidence) say humans react. The justification is usually something like "I've done it for so long, it's natural to me now."

Things that work against your body's natural reactions are never "natural." They may be habitual, familiar from repetition when your instinctive reactions have not been initiated, but that doesn't make them natural. For instance, adopting a bladed boxer's stance because it "feels natural" works against the body's natural desire to square itself to the target and crouch as it lowers its center of gravity. That special learned stance might be comfortable, but it's not likely to be what works when your threat responses have been activated.

Habitual? Yes. Familiar? Certainly. Natural? Probably not.

Key points to remember

1) The body's natural reactions are a function of neurology and physiology, and don't vary all that much from person to person.

2) The natural instinctive reactions cannot be trained away, but they can be controlled or converted through training.

3) The visible external reactions are markers of the underlying internal reactions.

4) These reactions happen when suddenly confronted with a lethal threat, not so much when you know something is going to happen. Training based on pro-active action does not activate these reactions, no matter how "stressful" it is.

5) Your training needs to take these into account if you are to be efficient, because fighting them with non-intuitive techniques (which may not even be possible to perform in a real incident) is inefficient.

[13]Taflinger

[14]Bowen, R.A.: "Hormone Chemistry, Synthesis and Elimination", Colorado State University. http://www.vivo.colostate.edu/hbooks/pathphys/endocrine/basics/chem.html

[15]Black, Harvey: "Investigators Pinpointing Fear's Activity in the Brain". The Scientist, June 22 1998. http://www.the-scientist.com/?articles.view/articleNo/18978/title/Investigators-Pinpointing-Fear-s-Activity-in-the-Brain/

[16]Grossman, Dave: "The Physiology of Close Combat", http://www.killology.com/art_psych_combat.htm

[17]Silverthorn, D.U.: "Human Physiology: An Integrated Approach", ISBN 0321541308

[18]Eagleman, David M.: "Human time perception and its illusions", http://www.ncbi.nlm.nih.gov/pmc/articles/PMC2866156/

[19]Hancock, P.A. and Weaver, J.L.: "On time distortions under stress". Theoretical Issues in Ergonomics Science Vol. 6, No. 2, March–April 2005, 193–211. http://peterhancock.cos.ucf.edu/on-time-distortions-under-stress/

CHAPTER 8

MAKING DECISIONS EFFICIENTLY

When I watch videos of actual surprise attacks, one of the things that stands out is how slowly people respond. I'm not talking about how slowly they move or shoot, but how slowly they get from the point where the attack starts to the point where their response is initiated. There is usually a gap – some call it a reactionary gap, I prefer the term "time sink" – between the points of attack and response. In many cases that gap is the biggest time waster of the event.

In contrast, I've taken a number of shooting classes where a majority of the instructional time was focused on things like learning to draw the gun from the holster fractions of a second faster. I've been told that the faster I can get the gun out of the holster, the faster the attack will end. There was a time I believed that, but viewing the objective evidence from many incidents has convinced me that it's not strictly true.

Don't get me wrong; learning to efficiently draw your pistol is certainly important. Having to fumble around or getting the gun snagged in the process will certainly waste valuable time. In this book, though, you'll note that the chapter you're reading comes well ahead of the chapter on drawing your pistol. Why?

Because the athletic skill of drawing the gun is secondary to efficiently processing information prior to making the decision to draw. The more efficiently you can make the decision to draw the gun, the sooner you'll be out of danger regardless of how fast your draw is.

The athletic skill of drawing the gun is secondary to efficiently processing information prior to making the decision to draw.

Drawing your pistol smoothly and quickly is certainly important, but so is efficiently determining that you need to!

AWARENESS AND PERCEPTION

Believe it or not, there are things going on around you right now that you don't know are happening. More precisely, you're not aware that those things are happening, in the sense of using the cognitive portions of your brain, affording you the ability to think about what's happening.

You may not know that these things are happening, but your brain does. Confusing? Yes, until you understand that your brain is constantly collecting and analyzing data about everything around you without you knowing it. It perceives what's going on and is making decisions about what to bring up to the level of awareness so that you can actively think about them.

For instance, if you're sitting in your comfortable chair reading this book and a bomb were to go off behind you, your brain would perceive the explosion a fraction of a second before you became aware of it. This was brought home to me one day when I was looking at pictures of a mortar attack that happened in Iraq's civil war. There were four people – insurgent fighters – milling around in a building, attending to various tasks. There was a photographer shooting pictures of them, and got one frame just as the mortar shell penetrated the wall and detonated. In the picture you can see the fireball just beginning to form at the same instant that a couple of the men are looking at the camera with completely normal facial expressions. Their bodies, however, were already starting to react to the sound and pressure wave of the expanding blast – evidenced by the presence of the external reactions we talked about earlier.

The men weren't yet **aware** that there was an explosion, in the sense that they had cognition or understanding of what was happening, but their bodies had **perceived** it and had already started to respond. It was a chilling picture because looking at it half a world away, I realized that I knew something that they didn't yet know when the shutter had snapped. I knew what was happening before they did. It is so illustrative of the concepts here that I think it's worth bringing up such a disturbing subject.

Your initial startle reactions – your natural reactions – happen because your brain perceives something that it categorizes as a threat, and that perception initiates your natural survival instincts. It's not until you become actively aware of the threat that you're able to recognize what's happened and decide how to respond. That awareness happens much more slowly than the perception.

WHERE DOES THE TIME GO?

Between your body's instinctive reactions that alert you to a threat and the point that you start to draw your pistol are two possible courses of action: one where you improvise a response and the other where you recall and perform a practiced skill.[20]

Improvisation in the heat of the moment

Someone who has never been in a lethal force situation or who has never thought about what he or she would do in response to a deadly attack will be forced to improvise their response. The body's natural reactions serve to alert the analytical functions of the brain (those cognitive processes), which then go to work on a solution. This takes time; while we think of our brains as being very fast it still takes time for the brain to gather the visual information it needs, analyze what's going on, then figure out the best course of action to take.

What kinds of things might the brain have to do? Well, first it has to figure out where the threat is; then it has to deduce what the threat is doing, if it's moving, if the correct response is to use lethal force; then has to direct the muscles to begin the draw stroke, figure out exactly where on the threat to shoot, then actually align the gun on target and stroke the trigger. This doesn't even begin to account for all the other stuff in the middle: Is there an innocent behind the target? Is he holding a hostage? Is he turning and changing the level of precision needed? All of this has to be analyzed and considered in the response. Doing all that takes valuable time.

Interestingly enough, the improvised response is always going to be an intuitive one, because your body is not going to decide to do something that it doesn't do easily; it's not going to choose to do something that doesn't work well with itself.

If you've trained in techniques that are non-intuitive, that don't work well with what your body does naturally, in the compressed time frame of a criminal attack your brain is likely to throw that training out and improvise a response that will be more in line with its natural reactions – a response that is more intuitive.

Where's the evidence, you say? It's on video. Objective video evidence of criminal attacks where shooting was involved almost invariably show the defender, regardless of prior instruction or experience, adopting a squared-off stance and extending his arms equally in front of him with the gun on his centerline (in and parallel with his line of sight). That improvised response works well with the body's natural reactions of orienting to the target, dropping the center of gravity, and increasing resolution in the center of the field of view. The improvised response is always going to be an intuitive one.

The expert reacts to a stimulus, recognizes what the correct course of action is, then responds in an automated way.

As I said, improvising a response like this takes time and it's time you can often see in the videos. A classic one I saw shows a police officer stopping a van at night. He nonchalantly walks up to the driver's door when suddenly a large stainless pistol comes out the window pointing right at him. (It's almost like a cartoon; I half expected to see a little "bang" flag pop out of the muzzle!) Luckily the criminal's first round is a dud, giving the officer time for his body's natural reactions to start: his center of gravity drops and his hands come up into his line of sight, and the reaction is so complete that his hands try to swat the gun out of the way as a live round discharges.

By this time the officer has moved toward the side of the van and out of the immediate line of fire. He stands there for almost a full second before his cognitive mind figures out that he really needs to be shooting. He draws his own gun and returns fire as the bad guy speeds off. The officer's aim is good, and the driver crashes into a power pole perhaps fifty yards away. The attacker will later be pronounced dead at the scene.

The second or so that it took for his conscious thought processes to improvise a response could have cost the officer his life. Could he have done anything to make those thought processes faster, to reduce the time it took for his brain to improvise his response?

Yes, and experts do it every day.

How experts make decisions

There is a growing body of work, such as that of Gerd Gigerenzer,[21] that explains how people who are well-versed in a subject – experts, we call them – make decisions. As it happens, they've learned to make a connection between things they perceive and their decisions.

Central to that decision making skill is the fact that the brain is very good at associating outcomes with circumstances. Even if you're not aware of it, your brain is constantly evaluating the data flowing into it and quickly coming to decisions about what to do. It does this because it's been trained to do it.

Take, for instance, driving a car. Remember when you first started to drive, how much stuff there was to do? You had to keep the vehicle in the lane, moderate the throttle, operate the clutch and gear shift, brake when appropriate (but not so much that you skidded), use the turn signals, spin the wheel just enough to change its direction but not so much that you scraped the curb, and so on.

Now you do all that stuff (and more) without thinking about it; you have become an expert. Over time and given enough exposure to driving, your brain has become accustomed to all the inputs that come from the activity and has automated its responses.

Today you can drive down the road and if a soccer ball rolls out in front of you, you are very likely to stomp on the brake pedal before you actually think about the ball itself, let alone the child that is likely to be chasing it. That process has become automated; your brain has associated the need to stop the

Look at all the controls you use everyday just to get to work. How many of them do you have to think about to use?

Stomping on the brakes in an emergency isn't something you need to think about; through repetition and experience, it has become an automated response.

car with the act of hitting the brakes. You don't need to think about picking your foot off the accelerator pedal, moving it over to the brake pedal, and quickly pushing the pedal down with a maximum of force. You respond to an emergency and make decisions about how to deal with it in an automated way – the way of the expert.

In training this is often called a stimulus and response cycle. A stimulus occurs, your brain recognizes the stimulus, then responds to it. This cycle can be within your awareness, as the improvised response is, or within your much faster perception, as is the expert's response.

The expert reacts to a stimulus, recognizes what the correct course of action is, then responds in an automated way based on the course of action without having to devote cognitive thought to the response process itself. It's how decisions are made most efficiently.

Stimulus and automated responses

To make decisions that efficiently you need to automate your responses. That is, train in such a way that the choices you need to make occur without you having to think about it.

Many people, even some trainers, believe in trying to make shooting an "instinctive" process. That's wrong on several levels. First, instinctive things are physiological reactions, things that are done as direct consequence of a stimulus and cannot be trained away.

Second, even if we could magically make shooting a truly instinctive reaction, we wouldn't want to. A true instinctive response would have you pulling your gun and shooting your child if she startled you while you were reading the newspaper.

We can, however, automate our responses by training properly. By automate I mean relegate the nuts and bolts of our response to the non-cognitive parts of the brain. Some people rather crudely refer to this as "muscle memory," but the expert goes way beyond that.

The Combat Focus® Shooting course has a very good way of explaining this, and it's called the Warrior Expert Theory: Through frequent and realistic training, experts learn to use the power of recognition to respond to patterns of information more efficiently. Experts make use of the brain's ability to recognize a stimulus, recall the skills necessary, and then respond without needing cognitive thought once the decision to respond has been made.

It's important to emphasize that this process is automated, in the sense that the micro-managing of the response is done below your level of awareness, but not automatic (performed start to finish without your control). In plain language, the decision to shoot isn't automated, but the execution of that decision is.

Training for automated responses

The goal of becoming an expert is to build the mental links between recognition (your understanding that a threat exists) and response (your execution of the appropriate skill). The key to doing this, as I just mentioned, is frequent and realistic training.

The frequent part is pretty self explanatory, but it's the realistic part that trips up most people.

The first part of realistic training is choosing to train intuitive skills – those skills which work well with what your body does naturally. As I hope I've pointed out, non-intuitive skills are not the ones that your body is likely to choose when faced with a truly surprising lethal threat; that's one of the reasons why people often improvise a more intuitive response.

(Non-intuitive skills might work when the threat is anticipated or you're given some space of time in which to prepare. As I pointed out in the chapter on the body's natural reactions, the chemical changes that initiate those reactions are both specific and short-lived. Given even a small amount of time for preparation or time to wear off, those reactions might be diminished. The available data, however, shows that's not the way that most lethal threats happen in private sector self defense. That's why we're talking about the surprise criminal attack here.)

Since improvisation takes time, and your body is going to do what it does naturally anyhow (remember that you can't train your natural reactions away), why not start by adopting techniques that work with what your body is going to do anyway? That's both efficient and realistic.

I'll get more into specifics in the coming chapters, but here's an example: practicing a bladed stance with bent elbows is non-intuitive and therefore not realistic. A natural, neutral square-to-the-target stance is what your body wants to do when suddenly faced with a threat, and is therefore realistic.

Practicing a non-intuitive stance like this, one that is not congruent with the body's natural reactions, is not practicing realistically.

The second part of realistic training is to practice under the conditions you're likely to need to shoot. This doesn't mean you need fully-furnished shoot house with mannequins; it does mean that you need to practice at unpredictable distances and with varying size targets, and with shoot indications that are not known beforehand. We'll explore this in depth in the chapter on practicing realistically.

Ultimately, the goal is that, once you've made the decision to shoot, your intuitive response happens without your having to think about it. You shouldn't need to use your valuable cognitive resources to decide how much deviation control to use or how fast you should shoot or if you need to use your sights or even how precisely you need to shoot. Those things can and should be left to the non-cognitive parts of your brain, the parts that respond more efficiently. That's what the rest of the book is about.

[20]Pincus, Rob: "Counter Ambush Training", ICE Publications, 2013

[21]Gigerenzer, Gerd: "Gut Feelings: The Intelligence of the Unconscious" Penguin Books, ISBN 978-0143113768

CHAPTER 9

WHAT IS
PRECISION
IN DEFENSIVE SHOOTING?

You're looking at two targets, let's say of the IDPA variety where there is an eight-inch central circle representing the optimum defensive shooting area (what is usually called the "down zero" zone). On one target there are a half-dozen shots scattered inside the circle, while on the other those same half-dozen are in a tight little group in the middle of that circle. Which shows a better understanding of precision from the standpoint of a defensive shooting?

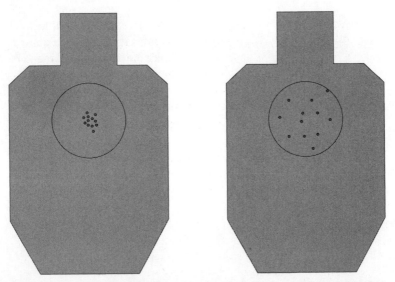

Which of these targets shows a better understanding of precision in defensive shooting?

Before you answer, remember that the goal in defensive shooting is to make your attacker stop using the least amount of your resources as possible – in other words, efficiently. Is taking the time and energy to achieve smaller groups really a mark of good, efficient defensive shooting?

I'd say "no." It certainly is a display of athletic shooting prowess, but it's not efficient because of the time and energy it takes to achieve that level of precision when it isn't needed.

WHAT IS PRECISION?

Many people use the terms "accuracy" and "precision" interchangeably, but they're not the same. In defensive shooting they represent two very different concepts, and it's important to understand those.

Precision, as we'll use it, refers to the area in which you need to place your bullets. In our IDPA target example, the precision needed is represented by the "down zero" circle. Every shot within that circle is worth exactly the same number of points as every other shot, and there is no bonus for hitting in the center of that circle rather that closer to the edge.

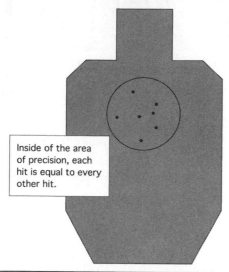

Inside of the area of precision, each hit is equal to every other hit.

In defensive shooting, the area of precision is similar in concept: it's that area in which each shot will contribute the maximum amount to stopping the attack. (We know, of course, that there are huge variables in the effect of any particular bullet, and the effect can vary with fractions of an inch of placement, but we also know that targeting vulnerable areas – such as the high center chest – will lead to the most rapid incapacitation by doing the maximum damage to the body's most vital functions.)

It's your job to recognize what that area is and recall the skills necessary to deliver that level of precision.

If you take nothing else from this discussion, take this: the target determines the precision needed, not the shooter!

The target (in the case of defensive shooting it's a criminal attacker) determines the precision needed by what is exposed. For instance, the bad guy could be crouching behind a car with only his head and shoulders showing. In that case, the area of precision is very different than if he were standing directly in front of you. The dictated area of precision varies, and the target is in charge. It's your job to recognize what that area is and recall the skills necessary to deliver that level of precision.

If your attacker – your target – changes position or alignment, the area of precision changes as well.

WHAT, THEN, IS ACCURACY?

Accuracy, on the other hand, is whether or not any given bullet you fire actually hits within the area of precision that you've recognized. If your shot hits within that area, it is accurate. If it doesn't, then it is not accurate. Accuracy is a digital concept; it is yes or no. Either you delivered the precision needed, or you did not.

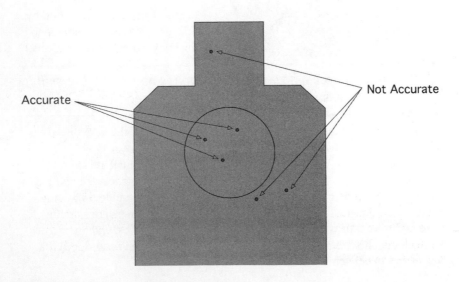

Accurate

Not Accurate

Think of a shooting match where you're facing the ubiquitous eight-inch falling steel plate. Any hit on that plate will flip it over and gain you points, but any miss will leave it standing there to mock you (I speak from experience). If you hit that plate, it doesn't matter where you hit it; a hit is a hit is a hit. If the bullet connects with the steel, the plate will go down and you get the credit.

If you deliver the amount of precision dictated by the target, you win. If you don't, you lose. Accuracy is whether you hit the target as it has been defined by itself.

You can't be "more accurate"

Because accuracy is a state of achieving the required level of precision, there is no such thing as "more accurate" or "less accurate"; either you hit where you intended/needed to, or you didn't. This is a hard concept for many people to understand, because the standard for decades has been to learn to shoot more and more precisely: into smaller and smaller areas. Once you realize that you don't get to choose the area of precision, you'll understand that **your job is to simply place your bullets into the area that the target has determined**. The measurement of your success is whether you were able to. Precision is best thought of as accuracy inside of a specified area.

Can you choose to shoot to a greater level of precision? Yes, you certainly can – at least, on the training range. The problem is that it doesn't make any sense to do more than the target requires because you have to give up something else to do it.

For instance, you could certainly choose to shoot each of those steel plates dead center rather than accepting a hit anywhere on their surface. The results – the toppling of the plate – are identical in each case. Since your job is to recognize the level of precision that the target requires, choosing to shoot to a greater level of precision than what is needed does nothing for your ability to understand the target.

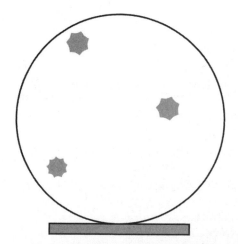
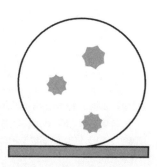

Shooting to a greater level of precision than needed isn't practicing realistically; shooting to a greater level of precision because the target demands it is.

Once you've achieved the necessary accuracy,
any attempt to shoot more precisely is wasteful.

If you want to shoot to greater levels of precision, it's better to use targets that demand a greater level of precision. Then you get the practice not just of delivering the accuracy needed, but also recognizing the precision required. The two go together: your recognition of the precision required should trigger your recall of the skill necessary to achieve it.

THE REALITY OF STOPPING THE THREAT

If you are to stop your attacker, you have to accept that you're going to need to do damage to his vital organs and functions. You need to do the right kind of damage, and you need to do enough of it.

It's possible to cause the right kind of damage, but not enough of it; it's also possible to cause a lot of damage, but not of the right kind. You have to do both!

Is it likely that a single shot will do enough instantaneous damage to cause your attacker to stop? No, it's not. There are certainly those rare occasions where a single shot might do that, but that's not something you can depend on. You must acknowledge that stopping a threat will most likely require a quantity of damage that can only be obtained with multiple shots. Those shots will stand the best chance of doing so when they land within the area of precision that the target has dictated.

In a defensive shooting incident, the target predetermines the precision necessary not actively, but simply because of its construction: physiology, or where the important bits are located. Human physiology is pretty static, but the precision needed to affect it changes because the target (and you) operate in three-dimensional space. The shape of the physiological target changes with angle, height, position, and posture.

ACCURACY IS EFFICIENT!

Let's say that in a particular incident the precision needed, the area of maximum damage by any given bullet, encompasses an area the size of your outstretched hand. To be accurate, your shots would have to land inside of that area. (Don't misunderstand: the damage that inaccurate shots do may in fact be valuable and disruptive, but that damage isn't equal to that caused by the shots which land in the target area itself.)

Since your job is to do rapid and significant damage inside that area, and inaccurate shots don't do as much of it as accurate ones, they waste the time, energy, and ammunition that you expended. In other words, inaccurate shots are inefficient. Remember that inefficiency simply gives the bad guy more time to hurt you or the people you're protecting.

Here's the important thing: once you've achieved the necessary accuracy, any attempt to shoot more precisely than that needed by the target is wasteful too. If you accept the idea that shots which land inside of the area of precision dictated by the target are doing the maximum damage already, and that each hit is going to be roughly equal in value to every other hit, then trying to place shots closer together (shooting to an artificially inflated level of precision) doesn't do you any good. It does, however, waste time. What is a wasted resource? Inefficient!

This is why I pointed out that you should be focusing on efficiency rather than effectiveness. Things that are efficient are by definition effective, but effective things are not necessarily efficient. Delivering an artificially inflated level of precision, that beyond which the target demands, requires additional time and effort that may not be justified by meaningful effect on the attacker. This extra time and effort for any given shot is wasted, and could be better used in delivering another shot (doing more damage). The expenditure is inefficient.

Randomized practice helps you to learn to recognize what must be shot, recognize the precision that it dictates, and then recall the physical skill of deviation control to get your hits.

If you're already hitting all shots in the heart, for example, attempting to concentrate those shots in the left ventricle doesn't really achieve anything additional. You're already doing the maximum damage, and the extra time and effort that it takes to achieve this unneeded level of precision could be better spent shooting more and doing more damage.

Once the precision threshold has been reached, it's the number of shots, not how close to each other they land, that will determine the damage that

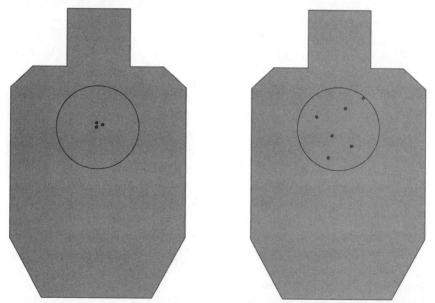

To make your attacker stop, you need to do more damage. Shooting additional accurately-placed rounds does that more efficiently than shooting fewer shots to an arbitrarily greater level of precision.

stops the threat. The more rounds that hit inside the area of precision, the faster your threat is going to stop.

Making your shots accurate, meaning that they all land in the area of precision dictated by your target, is the most efficient way to stop the threat. Since everything in defensive shooting is (or should be) evaluated by its effect on the target, and higher levels of precision beyond the threshold required are not likely to result in greater effect, attempting to do so during an incident is wasted time and effort.

You either are, or are not, accurate; there is no such thing as "better" once the threshold has been crossed. Not being sufficiently accurate is inefficient, and attempting to deliver a greater level of precision than the target dictates is inefficient as well.

REMEMBER RECOGNITION?

In a previous chapter I talked about the meaning of expertise – what it is to be an expert, in this case about defensive shooting. Through frequent and realistic training you can use your brain's ability for recognition to make more efficient decisions. This is true for the precision that the target dictates.

If you're attacked you'll have a lot of decisions to make in a very short period of time. One of them comes after the could-should decision (the one where you decide that lethal force is necessary): exactly what it is that you're going to shoot.

You already have a little foreknowledge about the level of precision that might be necessary, simply because you know a little about anatomy. You'll have to wait to find out exactly what precision the target dictates, because you don't know what part of his anatomy the attacker will present to you. Precision may be dictated by the target, but it has to be

Which target will you be asked to shoot next? There are several levels of precision needed on this target, and it's only when the command is given that you will know – recognize – what level of precision the target is demanding. That's realistic practice!

recognized by you, the shooter. Your target is in control of the circumstances, but you are in control of your response to those circumstances.

If you train with random-sized targets, called randomly by a partner, you will start to develop that recognition and recall sequence necessary for expert-level response. If you don't know which target is coming next, you won't know ahead of time the level of precision it dictates. Training in this manner allows you to get experience in quickly determining the level of precision, and then recalling the skills (control over the gun) that allow you to place accurate shots.

This kind of randomized practice helps you to learn to recognize what must be shot, recognize the precision that it dictates, and then recall the physical skill of deviation control to get your hits. This process is far faster than cognitive thought, and is much better suited to adapting to the rapidly changing environment of an attack.

I'll go into this in more detail in the chapter on practicing realistically.

RAPID, MULTIPLE SHOTS

As I've already mentioned it is unlikely that a single shot is going to take your attacker out of commission. It is multiple shots, delivered quickly, that are most likely to do that job.

As it happens, delivering the necessary accuracy for the first shot and for each additional shot both require the same physical skills: command over the gun that reduces the area in which the bullets might land. That concept is called deviation control, which I'll talk about in detail in the next chapter, but for now it's enough to point out that in order to hit a smaller target, or one further away, you need to apply more control over the gun. If you're going to fire more than one shot (and remember that you are likely to need to do so) you'll have to apply that deviation control continuously as you shoot.

The difference is in continuity; if you know you're only going to fire one shot, you'll tend not to apply the necessary post-discharge control that sets you up for the next shot. If, on the other hand, you accept the possibility that you'll be firing more than one round, you will automatically apply the appropriate follow-through that keeps you on target. To deliver the level of precision needed by the target for the first and each additional shot, the basics – stance, grasp, trigger control, and all the rest – need to be consistent and continuous.

EXPANDING YOUR UNDERSTANDING OF PRECISION

When you consider that defensive shootings are dynamic and chaotic events, it becomes obvious that levels of precision cannot be exactly defined. Going back to the discussion about aiming for the heart, though it may be the very best route to target incapacitation it's probably not going to be practical to aim for it specifically while everyone (you and your attacker) is in motion – the likely state of a violent attack.

This is why precision from the standpoint of defensive shooting is impossible to define exactly. If an instructor folds a piece of paper in half and says "that's a good defensive group size," he's predefining something that may or may not have any basis in reality.

The level of precision that you recognize has to be that where any given bullet can be expected to contribute the maximum amount to stopping the attack. If your attacker is facing you directly, squared off to you, that area is probably going to be his high (upper) center chest. Shots in that area are likely to do significant damage to his ability to present a threat to you, and over time this has come to be accepted as the most reliable way to disable an opponent over a wide range of circumstances.

Note that I didn't say something like "an eight-inch circle in the upper chest area." The exact size of that area is determined by the physiology of the attacker; bigger people are likely to have bigger chest cavities, while on little runts like me that circle covers the shoulders. Applying the bigger guy's level of precision to me means that a lot of bullets would not be hitting in tremendously vital areas.

Are all hits really equal?

From a purely intellectual standpoint we know that a shot that actually hits the heart is probably more valuable than one taht simply hits a lung. However, it's not efficient to try to place shots at that level of precision with a handgun during the kind of chaotic, threatening incident we're talking about. It's entirely possible that both you and your attacker will be moving – either trying to attack (him) or keep from being attacked (you).

Instead you settle for a level of precision that will do an historically reliable job of stopping your attacker while at the same time actually being achievable in the chaos of the attack. This level of precision has to accommodate not just the physiology of the attacker, but the reality of the environment and of the circumstances under which you're shooting.

This is why it's important to understand that precision is **recognized**. The exact circumstances of your attack will all contribute to your recognition: how he's standing relative to you, if there are intermediate barriers that will absorb or deflect your bullet, the assailant's size, and more all have a part to play in the determination of the precision dictated by the target – and they might change during the course of your defensive action.

The most vital part that can be reliably hit is the level of precision necessary. If the attacker turns slightly to one side, then your recognition changes as his vital area narrows slightly. If he ducks behind a trash can, the area of precision changes again.

As I've already pointed out, trying to achieve a greater level of precision than required in any specific situation is inefficient (using more time and effort), and may not even be possible given the short time frames of the typical attack.

Will becoming a 'better' shooter help?

Seeking artificially high levels of precision, beyond what the target requires, during an incident is counterproductive to efficient defensive shooting. Working to simply become a better shooter, in other words spending time

What's the precision this target is dictating?

learning to deliver artificially high levels of precision, may not be the best way to train to survive violent encounters.

As we've seen, there isn't a single level of precision appropriate to all encounters. Your need for accuracy (actually hitting the target area) doesn't change, but the recognized precision (which tells you how carefully you need to shoot) certainly does.

Your highest efficiency in training is attained by focusing your efforts on being able to deliver appropriate levels of precision – no more, no less – on demand, as quickly as you can, without cognitive thought as to the application of your skill. The recognition of the precision needed should trigger a recall of the skills necessary to achieve it.

Allowing yourself to shoot the same target over and over, focusing only on speed, is not practicing realistically. You have nothing to recognize (or, more precisely, nothing to practice recognizing) because the precision needed has been statically and arbitrarily predetermined. Your drills become a choreographed and overly mechanical test of muscle control, and you end up focusing on the anticipation of the shot as opposed to the recognition of the need to shoot.

In order to build the recognition and associative recall ability that makes for expertise, you must reduce anticipation by including options in your drills. Those options must be presented randomly, forcing the you to recognize the precision needed and then recall the necessary skills to make accurate shots inside of that area.

It's the association of the recognition and the recalled skill that forms the links necessary for this highly efficient decision making to happen. That can't occur unless for any given drill there is more than one option, and it's presented randomly.

Any attempt to define a "good defensive shooting group," regardless of what the definition may be, dooms the process to failure because there is no recognition for you to have.

CHAPTER 10

BALANCE OF SPEED AND PRECISION

No matter how long you've been shooting, you've probably realized that to achieve greater precision (accuracy inside of a smaller area) you need to take more time. You also probably realize that if you shoot faster, taking less time, you'll give up some precision. That's the tradeoff in defensive shooting, and every situation has a different balance of speed and precision.

All defensive shooting (all shooting, really) is a balance of speed and precision, and always has been. I have hunting books written in the early 1960s where the author talks about this concept, so it's not exactly new. Thinking about it and systematizing it is new, however, and I believe that the Combat Focus® Shooting program was the first to approach it in a very analytical manner. The Balance of Speed and Precision has become one of the core concepts in that program because it is so important to becoming a more efficient defensive shooter.

WHAT IS YOUR BALANCE?

The optimum balance of speed and precision for any situation is going to be determined by a combination of you, your attacker, and your environment. Change any one, and your balance of speed and precision – you at your most efficient – will change as well.

Every shooting situation will have a different balance of speed and precision because the factors that affect that balance change. Even in the same (identical) scenario, two different shooters will have different balances because they have different capabilities and levels of competency. Even your own balance will change from day to day (or even hour to hour) as your level of fatigue changes.

Inside of your environment there are a wide number of variables that affect your balance, and realistic training helps you to experience and understand those variables. The size of the target, your distance from the target, the conditions under which you shoot, and even your anticipation of the need to shoot, all affect your balance of speed and precision.

The target dictates precision

The target, as we've already discussed at length in the previous chapter, dictates the precision needed. If it's a paper target, the scoring or hit zones are predetermined; for an attacker, his physiology and his position relative to you dictate the precision you need to deliver.

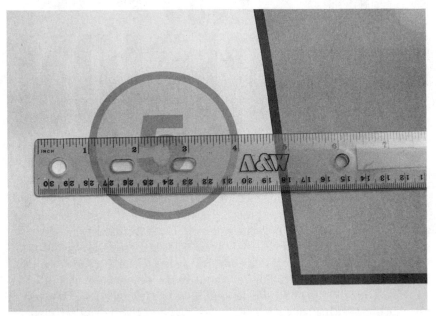

The target determines the precision needed; you can't change it, you can only recognize it.

Your job is to recognize the precision that the target dictates, but remember that you can't change it. You could decide to shoot to a greater level of precision, but I hope you now understand that it's inefficient (or even functionally impossible) for you to do so.

Your skill determines your hits

Your skill – or, more precisely, your application of your skill – determines whether you land the shots you need. In other words, your skill determines your accuracy.

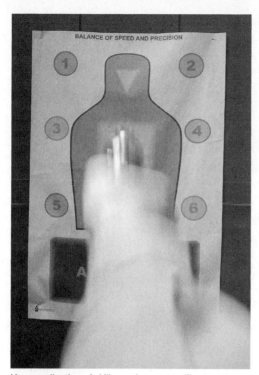

Your application of skill – such as controlling your muzzle deviation – determines whether you get the hits you need.

No matter how good a shooter you are, there is always some variability between where you intended the shot to go and where it actually lands. Some people have more deviation between aim and hit than others, but everyone's shots will deviate some. Controlling the amount of deviation will mean the difference between an accurate shot, one that hits within the target area, and one that doesn't.

Deviation control is the mechanism by which you exercise your application of skill, and it takes both time and effort. The amount of deviation control you need also varies; a large target area in close demands less deviation control than a smaller target area that is farther away. In those cases where the precision needed is rather loose, you can get away with less deviation control, which means that you can shoot faster. As more precision is needed you'll be forced to apply more deviation control (more skill) if you are to land accurate shots. That's going to take more time, which means you'll be shooting more slowly.

What causes deviation? You might not have good alignment on the target, whether using the alignment guides (sights) incorrectly or simply not having the gun in and parallel with your line of sight. You may not have mastered trigger control, and instead of staying steady the muzzle moves off target as the trigger is compressed (or off target completely when the hand relaxes as the trigger is reset). Some people blink just before the shot goes off, which disrupts the visual contribution to alignment. A loose grasp can contribute to excessive deviation, and if you're not solidly planted – feet not moving – when the shot breaks or if you're still in the process of extending your arms, deviation will increase.

Reducing deviation requires you to apply your skill: a proper sight picture (where appropriate), better trigger control, a strong unwavering grasp, and making sure that you have a solid stance before you press the trigger are some of the ways in which you do that. On the practice range this takes some concentration, and the reason to practice is to develop the ability to apply any given level of skill without having to actually think about it.

Your confidence determines your speed

It might seem odd that your confidence is in control of your speed, but it is. Your confidence in your own abilities determines how fast you'll shoot (unless you're shooting out of panic).

I'm not referring to confidence in terms of your personality or emotional makeup; instead I refer to the correlation between what you think you can do and what you really can, which is a product of your training and your practice.

Lots of people train under a specific set of circumstances constantly, never varying to any significant degree what they do. Same targets, same distance, same stance, same everything except trying to do it faster each time. This is the basis, in fact, for standards and benchmarks – an unvarying set of conditions under which objective measurements can be made.

Shooting the same choreographed drill under controlled conditions does not increase your confidence to recall skills on demand.

This idea comes to us from the competition side of shooting, where sports medicine meets scoring rings. It is based on the belief that shooting is a purely physical or athletic activity that needs to be quantified. This works only long as you can control the variables; since you can't control the variables of an attack, this approach leads to an unrealistic understanding of your own limitations.

Let's say that you train using a fixed course of fire. Since you've done it many times you know that you can draw and fire two rounds on target in, say, 1.5 seconds. Remember, that's when you know you're going to shoot, you know the distance, you're in a perfect stance, you know what your target is and where it is, and you've rehearsed the entire sequence in your mind.

You should always be shooting as fast as you believe you can get the hits.

Now do the same thing – only you're at the bus stop holding your child's hand and looking expectantly down the road when someone comes up behind you with a knife. You now have to process the threat through your mind, orient to the threat, possibly fire more than two rounds, and instead of that nice custom 1911 range gun on your hip you've got one of the ultra-light polymer pistols loaded with hard-kicking +P rounds in your pocket.

What's likely to happen? Your over-confidence and lack of realistic practice probably results in trying to draw and shoot at the same rate you do your phenomenal double-taps on the calm shooting range. Ever shoot a lightweight pistol too quickly? Then you know what happens to your deviation control: it usually gets very poor.

You'll attempt to shoot too fast because you've not trained under conditions like those you just experienced. The result is greater deviation (reduced accuracy), which as we've already discussed translates to being inefficient.

Being under-confident also stems from not training realistically. For instance, always using your sights in practice because you "can" rather than you "need to." When the attack happens, you of course default to attempting to employ them, despite not being completely able to (body reactions) nor really needing to (target very close). Because you doubt your ability to shoot using the threat focus you're forced into, and you're taking time trying to line up your sights just like you do on the range, you'll end up shooting slower. Again, the response is inefficient: wasted time.

The way to get correlation between your skills and your confidence in those skills is to train in the conditions under which you expect to shoot. That means random targets and distances, under many different conditions, so that you can develop a mental spreadsheet of what you can do and what you need to do under any combination of factors. Having a good understanding of your actual ability is what will keep you from being under- or over-confident, shooting too slowly or too quickly. You should always be shooting as fast as you believe you can get the hits, and realistic practice is how you come to a fact-based belief under any given set of variables.

THINGS THAT AFFECT YOUR BALANCE

Not understanding the variables, the factors that affect your balance of speed and precision, and moreover not training under as many of them as possible, will give you an incomplete picture of your own abilities. It's that incomplete picture that causes people to shoot at some rate other than what their ability would allow, producing an inefficient response.

I mentioned above that there were a number of things that directly affect your balance of speed and precision. First, of course, is the size of the target: that area which you recognize as being the optimum for rapid and reliable incapacitation in your attacker, or that which is delineated for you on the paper target at the range.

Size of the target

It's deceptively simple: the smaller the target area, the more deviation control you need to apply in order to get your hits. The more control you need to exert, the more time and effort it's going to take. The larger the target area, the less deviation control you'll need to use to get accurate hits (those which fall within the recognized area of precision) and the faster you'll be able to shoot.

Delivering higher levels of precision takes time and effort, which is why it's important that you train to what the target requires, rather than training to some arbitrary standard. It goes right back to the confidence issue: shooting at artificially higher levels of precision than needed leads you to a lack of understanding about what you can actually do. That's a lack of correlation between what you can do and what you believe you can do.

Distance to the target

In handgun training it's fashionable to ignore distance to the target and instead focus on the size of the target. The rationale behind this is that as you get further away the target appears smaller, and therefore paying attention to the size automatically takes care of the distance as well.

That's not entirely true, for a couple of reasons. First is the psychological effect of distance; I've observed that if there is a small target at a very close distance, most students will think that's pretty easy to hit. Whether it is in reality isn't important, because the student believes it is and usually delivers the hit. There's a very real value to the belief in one's abilities, as the discussion about speed pointed out.

Take a larger target farther away, so that it appears to be the same size as the small target did up close, and I've found most students start to choke. There seems to be a fear about shooting at any sort of extended distance, as though it's some sort of esoteric skill that only "advanced" shooters are able to master. It's not true, of course, but as distance increases so does the student's anxiety level.

It doesn't take a lot of distance for that to happen, either. I've noticed that simply doubling the distance from, say, ten to twenty feet is enough to trigger some degree of performance anxiety in most students. (That's getting to be at the outside of the most likely engagement distances in defensive shooting, but

Distance to the target, regardless of size, makes a huge difference – much of it psychological – on the balance of speed and precision.

still well within plausibility based on Tom Givens' data; it therefore makes sense to do some training at those ranges.)

One of the interesting phenomena relating to the psychological effect of distance is that the more experienced shooters will tend to start compensating for an imagined bullet drop. (For those who are new to ballistics, the pull of gravity combined with air resistance causes bullets to drop in a smooth and predictable arc as they travel.) This is a concern with rifles at extended distances, but with handguns it usually doesn't start to make a huge difference in the point of impact until it gets out in the fifty yard range (a typical defensive load will hardly drop at all at twenty-five yards). Intentionally "holding high" happens to a lot of shooters even when the distances are well under twenty-five yards, and often leads to rather substantial difference from where they thought the bullets would land.

Finally, the other major issue with target distance is that deviation increases as the range increases. Any amount of muzzle movement from the point of aim is magnified by distance, and the control that makes hits at ten feet is insufficient at twenty. At close distances reducing the target size requires an obvious increase in deviation control, but at extended distances the amount of control required is more than the apparent size of the target might indicate. Only training at these varying distances, ideally up to the outside edge of plausibility, will acquaint the shooter with the issues involved.

I've found that an occasional – and I do mean occasional – drill shooting at unreasonable distances (say, in the twenty-five to fifty yard range) will help cement these concepts in a student's mind. This should only be done after achieving competency at the plausible shooting distances, however.

The conditions under which you shoot

You, your attacker, and the environment in which the attack happens all dictate the conditions under which you'll shoot. The light level, temperature, whether it's raining, your level of fatigue, your familiarity with your gun, the surface on which you're standing, people around you – all of these will affect your balance of speed and precision.

Most of those should be self explanatory, as they affect you physically. Can you see your attacker clearly? Can you handle your pistol easily? Can you get a good grasp on the gun? Is it so cold you're shivering? So hot you're sweating? All of these, and more, will have an effect on you your balance of speed and precision.

Your familiarity with your pistol will impact your balance as well. If you're used to shooting a Glock but end up using an HK USP in self defense – having not shot it all that much – the difference in size, trigger operation (feel, weight and length of travel), sights, grips, and the location of the magazine release will all affect how you shoot. (It's worse if you spend most of your shooting time practicing, training, and competing with an autoloader but carry a five-shot revolver most of your waking hours!)

Environmental conditions – like being wet or cold – also affect your balance of speed and precision.

Imagine this fellow attacking you, but the playground filled with children – think that might influence how you shoot?

The perceived penalty for a miss

Imagine this scenario: you're walking through a park and round a corner toward the playground only to encounter a man threatening you with a knife. You smoothly draw your gun as you move laterally off the line of attack, and fire sufficient shots to cause your attacker to collapse. Good job!

Now, think about two different variations: same park, same attacker, same time of day, same weather, same playground, same everything – except in Variation 1 the playground is empty; in Variation 2 the playground is filled Is your balance of speed and precision going to change between those two scenarios? Are you going to shoot slower in one than the other?

For most people, the answer is yes. Shooting at an attacker against the backdrop of a full playground brings home the consequences of not delivering accurate shots to the target area: a miss might hit an innocent bystander. I'm not suggesting that you train for this by shooting around live targets – there are some trainers that do, and I consider it highly reckless – but understand that just because you can really whip those shots out when there's no penalty doesn't mean you can do so when something important is on the line. Your perception of the penalty for missing will affect how you shoot (and some-times whether you shoot at all).

Your anticipation of the need to shoot

Many years ago I was helping out on a hunt for a rogue and reportedly rabid bobcat at a local farm, sitting in a tree stand carefully surveying the area from which the animal would likely appear. Everything was ready; my rifle was in a position from which I could easily and without much movement bring it to my shoulder and fire. I'd been careful to make only the slightest and slowest movements with no sound. I was ready for anything, or so I thought.

I'd been there for nearly three hours when, out of the extreme corner of my eye, I saw a flash of movement in an open area well to my right. As I reflexively turned my head to check, I saw with the snarling animal on the ground below me and perhaps ten yards away.

I've hunted all my life and have never experienced "buck fever" or any other sort of performance anxiety, but this time I was surprised by an animal that I was, frankly, scared of (a large, mean feline being something with which I'm not at all comfortable). I instantly realized that it was fully able to leap to my position and do significant damage to my person. I brought my lever action rifle to my shoulder, clumsily cocking the hammer on the chambered round, and as the butt neared my shoulder I quickly – too quickly – fired the shot. One round, one hydrophobic carnivore. The hit was a good one, but it wasn't exactly where I intended it to go. The mercifully quick kill was as much luck as skill.

When you don't know that you're going to need to shoot, when your anticipation is low, and it takes longer to generate the proper response.

By any standard I was ready to shoot; I was on a hunt, had my gun loaded and chambered, had set myself up for the fastest and easiest shot, and was aware of the area the animal should have been in. What I wasn't ready for was that particular shot under those particular conditions. My anticipation of the shot that came was low, even though my general state of readiness was high.

This anticipation of which I speak is the likelihood, in your mind, of having to shoot just before you recognize the need to shoot. You might be ready, you might have all kinds of general awareness, you may even have your pistol in your hand and prepped to stroke the trigger, but if the need to shoot happens in a different place or a slightly different time or under different conditions, your anticipation is low.

This is very different than competition shooting, for instance (which we'll talk about in a little more depth in a later chapter). In a shooting competition, the anticipation of the need to shoot is quite high – you know what the targets are, you know where they are, you know how far they are from you, and a number of other things. In that case your readiness and your anticipation are roughly equal, and it takes less time for your mind to generate your response.

Now put yourself into the kind of ambush attack we've been considering throughout this book: you're trying to decide between mocha and espresso when you're suddenly attacked. Your state of general readiness is low, but your anticipation of the need to shoot is even lower. Unless you've trained under that kind of condition, your mind will take time to direct your response.

Your anticipation of the need to shoot – of needing to make any one shot – will therefore have a profound effect on your balance of speed and precision. In my case I fumbled what had been a well-rehearsed cock-shoulder-fire sequence; I didn't get a perfect cheek weld and I fired before the gun was well anchored on my shoulder. The shot worked, but the deviation was more than I had expected. The low anticipation of the need to shoot, even with my high state of readiness, had dramatically affected my balance of speed and precision. If the animal had been a little farther away I might have missed him entirely.

The anticipation of the need to shoot is as much a caution as it is a training prescription. It's easy to practice a choreographed drill on the range and turn in blistering performances. When you know ahead of time that you're going to be shooting a specific shot, your brain is primed for the performance; it knows what neurons to fire to get which muscles to do what tasks. When you don't know that you're going to need to shoot, when your anticipation is low, it takes longer to generate the proper response and that response is likely to not look like that well-rehearsed dance on the range.

This ties into the confidence issues we talked about earlier. Pretending that you're always ready because you've done the same old predictable drills over and over, and done them really well, is ignoring the reality of anticipation. In the chapter on practice we'll talk about some ways to spend your range time getting used to making better responses when you're not in anticipation.

CHAPTER 11

CAN YOU
– OR SHOULD YOU?

Should she draw and shoot?

*(**Note:** I am not a lawyer, and the following should not be considered legal advice. You should always seek the guidance of a lawyer in your own area, one who is conversant with the laws regarding self defense and the legal ramifications of the affirmative defense in court, before you make any legal decisions. There are criteria by which you might be judged in your actions, and I highly recommend that you take advantage of any courses that deal with the legalities of self defense in your area to familiarize yourself with them.)*

n the world of defensive shooting instruction there is always the "what if" discussion: "What if this happens, is it legal to shoot someone?" These kind of hypothetical questions are a traditional part of internet gun forums, to the extent that many of them have sub-forums just for such discussions.

Even in courses devoted to the legalities of self defense a lot of time is spent examining whether you can or cannot shoot someone. How close does someone need to get before shooting is allowed? What kinds of weapons constitute a threat that would excuse shooting? Big vs. small? Many vs. one? Young vs. old?

Don't get me wrong; all of those questions are valid and the answers are important to understanding the application of law in self defense cases. Knowing legal concepts such as the affirmative defense and what burdens it puts on you as a defendant in court is a vital part of your defensive training.

It's also important to understand that shooting a threat may very well lead to his death. While you never, ever shoot with the intent to kill, you do shoot to stop someone from killing you. Very often the result of that fight-ending action is the death of the attacker. This makes the decision to use your gun a very (pardon the pun) grave one: you may end up justifiably taking the life of another.

JUST BECAUSE YOU CAN, DOESN'T MEAN YOU SHOULD

From a philosophical standpoint, our laws are set up to recognize the reality that sometimes it's necessary to shoot, and possibly kill, someone in order to save your own life or the life of another innocent person. That's the idea of the affirmative defense, which is the basis for any claim of legitimate self defense: yes, you shot him, but you had an excusable reason for doing so.

Things have changed! Has her need to shoot changed as well?

A self-defense shooting can easily become the most expensive thing you'll ever do in your life – regardless of the circumstances.

In other words, there are situations under the law where you can shoot someone.

That doesn't mean you always should, however. Regardless of any local requirements for you to retreat unless otherwise unable, shooting someone should be reserved for those situations where you really need to – when there is no other recourse.

This isn't a defeatist attitude, nor am I saying that you must cower in fear. It is an attitude that reflects the fact that shooting another human being – even a lifetime criminal who is no good to society – will change your life. It will cost you money, time, reputation, and friendships. A criminal defense might cost you hundreds of thousands of dollars.

This kind of legal analysis is not something you're likely going to have time to do during an attack.

Even if you're cleared of criminal charges, the attacker's family might decide to press a civil suit against you, which is a common happening in today's world. Again, think tens of thousands of dollars, at a minimum.

Shooting someone should always be reserved for those situations where it's really necessary.

HOW DO YOU KNOW IT'S REALLY NECESSARY?

In the legal portions of many self defense classes are taught such concepts as ability, opportunity, and jeopardy – the three generalized criteria by which the use of lethal force is usually deemed justified. You need to know those things ahead of time so that you understand fully not just where you're allowed to use lethal force, but also some of the situations you aren't.

That kind of legal analysis is not something you're likely going to have time to do during an attack, however. In the heat of action, instead of focusing on whether you can use lethal force I believe it's better to focus on whether you need to.

It's possible, perhaps even likely, that when you really need to shoot there won't be enough time to run through that the legal analysis that answers the question "can I?" Your attacker appears suddenly, you see a known and articulable threat to your life, and you respond appropriately. That's the very situation for which our laws are made: when your life is in immediate and otherwise unavoidable danger and you must make a decision now.

Knowing ahead of time the kinds of attacks to which lethal force is appropriate and deciding under what circumstances you would and would not shoot will lay the groundwork for responding efficiently and appropriately.

Don't misunderstand: you may be legally allowed to shoot someone at some point during an encounter. The totality of the circumstances may be such that, as the old saying goes, there isn't a jury in the world that would convict you. You may have met all the legal criteria.

None of that means you should exercise your trigger finger unless you need to. This is why a class in the legalities of the use of lethal force is so important.

The courtroom downside to "can I?"

One of the problems with focusing on the "can I" rather than "do I need to" comes when that jury starts looking at your case. There have been court cases (which you can find in the Journal of the Armed Citizens Legal Defense Network, available online) where someone was legally allowed to shoot his attacker (or he at least believed he was legally justified), but the jury looked askance at his decision.

Focusing on the "can I?" tends to look very much like searching for loopholes, legal technicalities to get a guilty person off. Whether that's right or valid is a discussion for another book, but in those cases where the shoot decisions weren't clear-cut, the defendants had a much harder time – sometimes requiring more than one expensive trial – clearing themselves.

As I see it, it's a lot easier to defend the claim that "I needed to, and here's why" than it is to defend "the law says I could, so I did." That's why I focus on the "should" rather than the "can."

"If it's a good shoot, I don't have to worry"

One comment I hear a lot when talking about the legal aspects of self defense is the idea that someone who has been involved in a "clean" or "good" shoot doesn't have to worry, because his innocence will shine through to protect him.

If you believe that, I have a bridge I'd like to sell you!

The trouble is that neither you nor I (nor the investigating officers) get to decide what's "clean" and what's not. This isn't to say that they can't choose to drop an investigation due to overwhelming evidence or lack thereof – they certainly can – but not every self-defense case is absolutely clear-cut. There

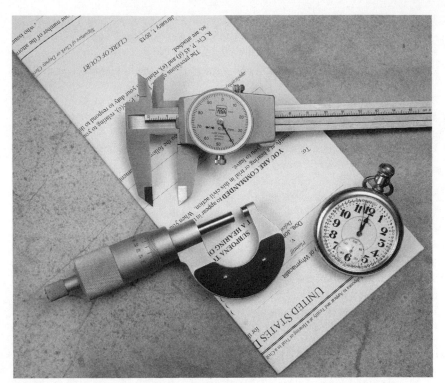

If you're the defendant, this is probably how it seems your testimony is being evaluated.

are many instances of legitimate defensive shootings where the evidence wasn't completely clear, those situations then being exploited by a politically-motivated prosecutor. I'll refer you to the back issues of the ACLDN Journal,[22] which chronicles several such cases.

Ultimately it's only the trier(s) of the facts – the jury, or the judge in a bench trial – that can definitively declare your case to be clean or not. In my state, a Grand Jury makes the first decision, and if they say it isn't "clean" it then goes to trial where you have the opportunity for a jury of your peers to make the final decision. In a trial someone else will be scrutinizing your act of self defense, and you'll be paying a lawyer huge sums of money to present your case in a favorable light.

If you remember nothing else, remember this: what looks clean to you or me may not look that way to a person who doesn't understand self defense. Even if you explain it in detail they may still not understand, especially if they're weighing your explanation against someone else who is trying to convince them of the opposite.

A criminal defense attorney I know is fond of saying that self defense is determined by inches and seconds. What seems perfectly fine to you may be interpreted completely differently by people who are looking at those inches and seconds in great detail and with the dual luxuries of time and undivided attention.

AFTER YOUR EARS STOP RINGING

It's after the incident that you need to be able to articulate why you did what you did. This is where your education in the legalities of self defense become important, as they help you understand why the law allowed you to respond with lethal force.

It's important, whether you shoot or not, that you get your own call into the 9-1-1 center as soon as you can. Though it's not, to the best of my knowledge, legal proof of innocence, investigators often take the stance that the first person to call in is the victim.

This is particularly true in those cases where a gun was drawn and for whatever reason shots were not fired. The bad guy gets to a phone first and says you assaulted him with a gun; minutes later your call comes in and you say he attacked you with a rock. Which one is more believable at that moment?

Call into 9-1-1 and first tell them your location – address and important landmarks. Then say that you need the police, that you were forced to shoot someone in self defense, and that the attacker is down and needs medical attention. Then describe yourself: height, weight, clothes, distinguishing features. This is so that officers will be able to instantly identify the good guy when they get on scene.

When they arrive, make sure that you're not holding your pistol in your hand! Either holster it before they see you, or put it down and step away. The last thing you want is for an officer to get out of his car at a shooting scene and see you holding a gun. They don't see the halo we all believe we wear; they see a guy with a gun and a guy on the ground leaking bodily fluids. This is not a situation in which you want to be mistaken for a threat!

Tell the officers only that you were attacked, that you were forced to shoot in self defense, and that you will "sign the complaint" (the actual legal version of "I'll press charges"). Be sure to point out any evidence (attacker's weapon, signs of a scuffle, indications on your person that you were attacked, etc.) so that it isn't missed in the investigation (or so that it doesn't magically stick to an accomplice's fingers and be taken from the scene. It happens.).

Be sure to point out any witnesses as well. People have a tendency to wander off, particularly if they're of the "I don't want to get involved" mentality. Make sure the officers know who can corroborate your story.

Once that's done, it's time to exercise your right to remain silent. In other words, stop talking! Don't give any more detail about how the incident happened or why you did what you did. Human memory is a fragile thing, especially in the midst of a traumatic incident, and you want to avoid saying anything that might be used against you later. You might think you've made an innocuous comment that later proves to be a large point of contention when it doesn't exactly match the objective evidence – or eyewitness testimony.

A good course of action, suggested by experts in the field, is to say something like "I know this is a serious situation, and you'll have my full cooperation as soon as I've had a chance to speak with counsel. I'm sure you can appreciate the gravity of my position." This is likely to pretty close to what

Make sure you're the first to call 9-1-1, whether you shot or not.

those same officers have been taught for those instances when they themselves are involved in an on-duty shooting, and serves as one more indication to them that you are, in fact, the innocent party.

This procedure ensures that you've given them the vital information they need to start their investigation, while at the same time exercising (and protecting) your rights against self-incrimination.

How you interact with the police after you've been involved in a shooting, how you articulate why you did what you did, and how well the forensic evidence is preserved will all be parts of how the jury decides whether you were justified or not. It's in your best interest to not screw any of that up.

MAKE USE OF EXPERT RESOURCES

I'll repeat what I said at the top: I strongly recommend that you get appropriate instruction in the legal aftermath of a defensive shooting. The premier source for educational material on the topic is the Armed Citizens Legal Defense Network (www.armedcitizensnetwork.org).

Famed instructor Massad Ayoob travels the country teaching what is probably the best course available on the legal issues of self defense. Called MAG-20, you can find it on his schedule at www.massadayoobgroup.com. (On a personal note, I consider MAG-20 to be so important that I suggest everyone who even contemplates using a gun for self defense take the course.)

---

[22]http://www.armedcitizensnetwork.org/our-journal, particularly the Larry Hickey case.

The foremost expert on the legalities of self defense is Massad Ayoob. His classes on judicious use of deadly force should be considered a "must" if you plan to carry a gun for self defense.

CHAPTER 12

MANAGING SCARCITY:
WHAT SKILLS DO YOU REALLY NEED?

You may not realize it, but you don't have unlimited training resources. Even if you are wildly, independently, obscenely wealthy your resources aren't unlimited. You have only so much time and so much energy, and even the biggest bank account can't change the fact that you have only so many hours on this planet.

Why do I mention this? Because the reality that your resources are limited affects your training decisions. You can't really train for everything that could possibly happen to you, because even if you had the money you certainly don't possess the unlimited time on this earth to do so. Your training resources, just like mine and everyone else's, are scarce – and managing that scarcity is critically important to your defensive preparations.

WHAT'S POSSIBLE?

There are all kinds of things that are possible in this world, and I mean

Which is more likely – this scene, or North Korean paratroopers?

possible in the sense that the laws of physics don't preclude them from happening. For instance, as you sit reading this paragraph it's entirely possible that a platoon of North Korean paratroopers could land in your neighborhood and take you (and everyone in the vicinity) hostage, in exchange for a large shipment of wheat to their country to aid in feeding their starving millions. Again, there is nothing in the laws of physics that would render this impossible; but let's face it, it's pretty darned unlikely.

If you'd spent all your training time preparing for a North Korean paratroop invasion, however, you'd likely be ill-prepared for dealing with the knife-wielding guy that came around the back of your parked car while you were busy getting groceries from the trunk. Training for the myriad number of things that are merely possible is a waste of your resources because it can leave you with serious gaps in your ability to deal with those things that are far more likely to occur.

If you're going to make the best use of your scarce training resources, you need to first focus on those things that are likely to happen: things that are probable.

PROBABLY BEATS POSSIBLY!

Probable things are those events that have some level of mathematical expectation tied to them. In other words, they are things that have happened to others in similar situations frequently enough that it's likely you could face them yourself.

It's these probable events to which you should devote the bulk of your training and practice. I mentioned the work of Tom Givens previously; his research shows some commonalities that serve to greatly define what is probable. For instance, it's likely that you'll be surprised by the attack, that you'll be between three and five yards from your attacker, that you'll be standing, and that you'll be shooting using both hands with the gun in your line of sight.

Your training time, money, and effort are most efficiently used by spending a majority of those resources learning to respond to that kind of situation: an ambush attack (one that you didn't know was coming), within those distances and under those conditions. As I mentioned at the start of this book, those skills will certainly be usable in those cases where you do have some fore-knowledge of an attack, but the reverse is not likely to be true.

Your probable may not be the same as someone else's

What's probable might vary a bit from person to person, because probability is somewhat dependent on the environment. For instance, someone who works on a farm beyond the suburbs faces a different set of daily risks than the urbanite who lives in a trendy housing development. There is some overlap, of course; a home invasion is a home invasion, and the fact that the farmer gets to town frequently and the city dweller goes to the country for recreation every so often means that the bulk of training for each of them is going to be very similar. Still, it's worth spending some time to understand the crime patterns in your area to help you decide how to bias your training. A well-informed local instructor should be able to help you with this; if he/she can't or won't, it's probably a good idea to seek better guidance.

Once you've developed the skills necessary to deal with the most probable events, you can expand the conditions under which your skills can be used beyond what is most likely: you can use them to deal with events that are plausible.

PLAUSIBILITY: THE OUTER LIMITS OF TRAINING

If possible things are those that could happen within the laws of physics, and probable things are those that are most likely to occur, plausible things are in between: those that have some historical precedence (they've happened occasionally) or for which it's logical to conclude that they could happen to you (the circumstances are such that the event could logically happen).

For instance, the probabilities are that you won't need to shoot with one hand – but it's plausible that you could be injured in one hand and need to shoot with the other, because it occasionally happens. It's also plausible that you could need your other hand to hold a flashlight or open a door or protect your child because the way you live your life, the environment in which you live, puts you in those situations with some regularity.

Plausible things might include shooting somewhat beyond the five yards where the best data says attacks usually happen, or being on the other extreme: in direct contact with your attacker (the techniques for which would fill another book). Some amount of your training, then, should be devoted to those plausibilities.

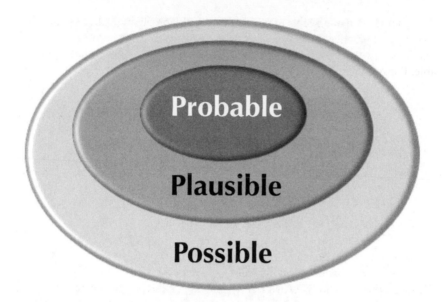

The efficient way to train, the one that makes the best use of your scarce resources, is to first focus on those things that are likely (probable) and only after that should you expand the range of circumstances under which you can use your skills to embrace the plausible. (Combat Focus® calls this the Plausibility Principle.)

IT'S NOT ALL ABOUT THE GUN

Remember that there is often a fine line between plausible (which is a good use of your scarce resources) and what is merely possible (a bad use of your resources). The problem is that the "merely possible" is often a whole lot of fun! Running in and out of live-fire houses, negotiating assault towers and shooting "tangos" on your way down is an adrenaline rush; after all, who doesn't like playing a real-life video game?

You're going to need a hard-nosed attitude with regard to your defensive training resources, because it's all too easy to get caught up in the Walter Mitty fantasyland of shooting instruction. Sadly, a large portion of the training industry is in fact devoted to things and situations that are distinctly implausible. It's up to you to recognize that and devote your scarce resources to being prepared for those things that you'll actually face.

What if you succeed in doing that? What if you actually manage (though I doubt it's really possible) to become very well prepared for all of the plausibilities in your life? Wouldn't it be okay to spend some "me time" playing hostage rescue?

No, I don't think so. Why? Because personal safety – the reason, hopefully, that you're reading this book – goes beyond shooting, beyond even hand-to-hand skills. If you expand the idea of personal safety, you'll probably realize that there are a whole lot of very likely life-threatening events that can happen to you and those around you. In fact, they're probably more likely

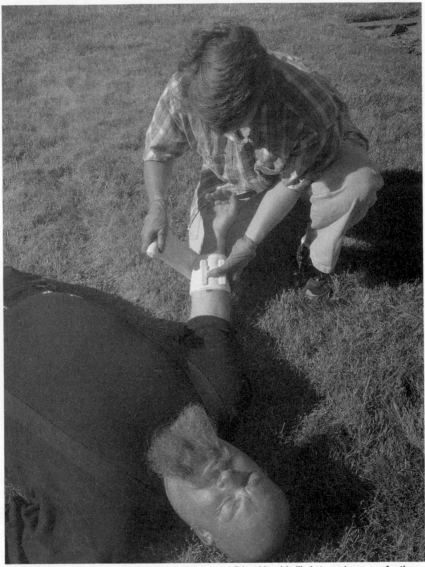

Spending time learning to deal with massive trauma (blood loss) is likely to make you safer than a weekend playing Special Forces soldier.

than you ever needing to draw your defensive firearm. Those plausible events require skills that don't include your defensive firearm.

What might some of these skills be? It's not often talked about these days, but defensive driving is becoming a more important part of daily life. The road rage incident you have on the way home is probably better handled by learning to drive away from the danger than by practicing shooting out your car window, for instance.

Take, for instance, severe trauma – the kind that results in massive blood loss. This kind of trauma can be caused by an accident in your workshop, your kitchen, or even while hiking. If you're a bow hunter, you're a slipped step away from a nasty broadhead wound. Knowing how to deal with this kind of trauma, and putting together a kit to help you do so, is probably more important than a weekend playing like you're on a SWAT team.

How's your generator? Your backstock of food? Do you have evacuation kits in your house if you're forced to flee from a devastating fire? Do you have proper extinguishers mounted around your house to help you prevent a little fire from becoming that big one from which you must escape?

If you spend a little time thinking about it, there are more threats to your life than just the bad guy with the switchblade. Spend some of your scarce training resources evaluating ALL of the plausibilities in your life, not just the ones that require shooting.

I realize that as a defensive shooting instructor I'm probably cutting my own throat by pointing this out to you, but integrity compels me to acknowledge that not every threat to your life is a shooting situation. Make your training decisions accordingly, but remember: your resources are not unlimited. Spend them wisely.

CHAPTER 13

FOUNDATIONS –
GRASP AND STANCE

Have you wondered why I started this part of the book talking about the body's natural reactions, before even stance and grasp and all the other things most instructors start with? Because the body's natural, instinctive reactions affect how and what you train – including grasp and stance.

THE BODY'S NATURAL REACTIONS GET PUT TO USE

We talked about the external manifestations of your body's reaction to a surprise and lethal threat. One of them was the lowering of your center of gravity; another was orienting to the threat (as well as fixating on it, which is part of the increase in resolution in your visual system). This is the position you're likely to find yourself in automatically when you recognize that you are under a threat.

As I pointed out, these are reactions that you can't train away; they are as close to a certainty as you're going to find in this area of study. The efficient thing to do is to work with them by structuring your techniques and training around them instead of trying (and failing, for the most part) to fight them.

STANCE

We know that one of the natural reactions is to square off to the target, so start with that. Stand so that your body is parallel to the face of your target, as opposed to being bladed like a boxer. Your feet should be somewhere around shoulder width apart and roughly on a line with your chest – one foot should not be markedly behind the other.

You'll find that once you're used to shooting in a natural position it's easy to adapt to other, less natural positions if the environment dictates. It's plausible that you could find yourself in a situation where you can't get your feet fully oriented toward the threat at the point you start shooting. That's fine; you can always work around the limitation.

If, however, you do all your training in an exaggerated, staggered-foot, or bladed stance and are forced to the other extreme – other foot forward and bladed the opposite direction –

Natural, intuitive stance puts shooter square to target, feet apart, lowered center of gravity.

you'll find it much harder to efficiently respond. Starting at a middle ground, so to speak, makes it easier to go to extremes than it is to spend all your time at one extreme and then try to go to the other when threatened.

LOWER YOUR CENTER OF GRAVITY

Before your body can move or mount a defense it's necessary to lower your center of gravity. This natural reaction can be duplicated in training by bending your knees and throw your buttocks backwards six to eight inches. This forces your upper body forward, and I tell my students to think of it as a shallow crouch – because that's what it most closely resembles. This is the fighting/movement position that humans adopt naturally when surprised. It's maneuverable and resistant to forces like punching and shoving. Coincidentally, it's also superb for resisting the recoil forces of a pistol.

With your torso and feet oriented to the threat and your center of gravity lowered, you're in an absolutely textbook position of natural reaction. It's from this natural, neutral position that we'll add the tool – the pistol – that we'll use to end the confrontation.

Lowered center of gravity is much like a shallow crouch.

GRASPING THE PISTOL

Remember that your training is going to be geared to delivering rapid, multiple, combat accurate hits on target; if your grasp is weak or intentionally light like a target shooting technique, it's going to make that task very difficult. Proper grasp within your limits of strength is the key to controlling your pistol's recoil, and the smaller and/or lighter your gun the more important it becomes.

Start the grasp with proper hand placement. The web (area between your thumb and forefinger) of the shooting hand should be placed as high as possible on the back of the grip, up against the tang underneath the slide; you should see a definite ripple of flesh if the grasp is high enough. This brings the bore line, relative to your hand, as low as possible and reduces the amount of leverage the gun has. In addition, it puts a solid, tensioned muscle underneath the tang, which in turn resists the backward cartwheeling motion of the gun. Together they serve to minimize recoil and muzzle flip to the greatest degree possible.

Remember the safety rules in the first chapter? Unless you're actually shooting, place your trigger finger straight along the frame just above the trigger.

Wrap the rest of your fingers around the grip, making sure that the top of your middle finger is in contact with the underside of the triggerguard.

The thumb should be relatively high, to make room for your support hand.

Depending on the size of the grip and your hands, there will be a gap of some size between the fingers and heel of the your palm that exposes the gun's grip panel.

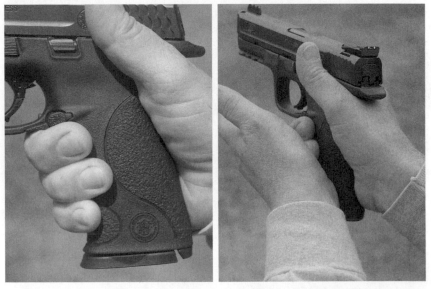

Into this area you're going to place the heel of your support hand.

Note that it's the heel of the hand, not the base of the thumb, that goes into that space! This has the effect of rotating the support hand forward, which increases its ability to help resist recoil.

Now simply wrap the fingers of the support hand over the top of the shooting hand, making sure that the forefinger touches the bottom of the trigger-guard.

Finish by layering (not crossing) the thumbs. Your shooting hand thumb should point forward, roughly in line with the barrel. (When I shoot one-handed I raise the thumb fairly high; I find that it cams the gun into my hand with a great amount of force, which increases control without needing to try to increase my finger pressure. I find the trigger finger stays more relaxed and trigger control is enhanced.)

The pistol grip is now encircled by muscle, with no gaps or weak points. This is the best way to control recoil, muzzle flip, and "squirming" in the hands.

Adjust your grip as necessary to get the specified contact points and make a mental note of how everything feels. It's that feeling that you'll want to replicate each time you grasp the gun.

THE READY POSITION

Once you've achieved a good grasp on the pistol bring it into what Combat Focus® refers to as the "high compressed ready" (HCR). The pistol should be close into your body, with your elbows tucked into your sides. The barrel should be pointing roughly at the target, or perhaps just a little lower, but never higher. The pistol should be somewhere around the base of your sternum, but no lower than your belly button.

Start with the High Compressed Ready, from which you'll be able to do a number of things with consistency.

This is a consistent position from which a number of techniques will originate. Remember what I said about consistency being a big part of efficiency? This is one of those instances where it shows itself; as you'll see, getting used to presenting the gun from this spot will pay dividends.

EXTENSION

From the high compressed ready and while in that natural, neutral stance simply extend the gun forward, into and parallel with your line of sight. Your arms should extend an equal amount, as opposed to one of the artificial, non-intuitive positions where one is bent and one isn't, or one is bent one way and one is bent another. (I'll have more to say about this in the next chapter.)

It's important that the gun comes into your line of sight and finishes extension while parallel to it. A large part of getting proper index on target, and settling the gun prior to firing the

Simply extend your arms equally to bring the pistol into and parallel with your line of sight.

The gun should be into your line of sight before you finish your extension.

shot, is making sure that that gun is not moving up or down relative to the target just before shooting. If you were to come into your shooting position from a "low ready" directly to the shooting position, the gun would still be moving upward as you reach full extension. You would then need to stop that upward movement and bring the gun back down on target before you could shoot.

The last 1/4 to 1/3 of the extension should be straight out to the target.

By bringing the gun immediately into your line of sight – at no more than roughly 2/3 of full extension – and finishing the extension by traveling parallel to your line of sight directly toward the target, you eliminate the need for a time-consuming elevation correction. It's a more efficient way of achieving a fast and sure index on the target.

THE VIDEO REALITY

When I look at objective evidence of brutal attacks, such as dashcam or surveillance videos, I consistently see that – regardless of the level of training – people adopt a shooting stance very much like I've outlined here.

The body's natural reactions dictate the physical positioning: lowered center of gravity, squared off to the threat, forward weight bias. Why the equally extended arms? That has a lot to do, I believe, with the way our visual systems have evolved to use tools (more about that in the next chapter).

My point is that what I don't see (and have never yet seen) is the exaggerated Weaver or Chapman-type stances that were once so common in defensive shooting instruction. As you've learned, the human body does very specific things when confronted with a lethal threat, and the available evidence supports the scientific contention that training doesn't really affect those things all that much.

If you know ahead of time that these are the things you are likely to do when surprised by a threat, doesn't it make sense to train and practice in ways that work with them? That's what intuitive skills are: skills that work well with what your body is going to do naturally. Doing anything else is non-intuitive and ultimately inefficient, both in terms of your training time and your responses to a threat.

CHAPTER 14

TRIGGER CONTROL
– THE KEY TO EFFICIENT SHOOTING

No matter which gun you've chosen, learning to grasp the gun properly and control the trigger can make the difference between hitting your target where you need to, or throwing a shot somewhere where it won't do much good.

CONTROLLING THE PISTOL STARTS WITH THE GRASP

Think about this: you're holding a gun that might weigh as little as 22 ounces. The trigger on that gun is likely to take six pounds of pressure (96 ounces; much more on a DA or DAO gun) to operate. It's pretty clear that 96 is more than 22, and that extra force needs to be controlled. It's going to take something to keep that 96-ounce force from moving the 22-ounce object around – and that something is your grasp.

A grasp that exceeds the 74-ounce (or more) difference between the trigger weight and the gun's weight is what you need to stop trigger-induced movement in the gun. That's not going to happen with a weak target-shooting grasp.

The pressure that you're able to exert in your grasp is what will hold the pistol steady when you shoot. Exerting the right amount of pressure, every time you draw the gun, is important to learn – and, as it happens, it's actually pretty easy: exert as much pressure as you can without causing the gun to wobble.

Here's how to find and practice your grasp pressure: get a proper grasp on the pistol, then extend your arms equally, straight out, as far as you can. Now squeeze with both hands as hard as you can, until you start to tremble from the effort. Now ever so slightly release the pressure just enough to stop the trembling, but no more. The resulting pressure you now feel is what you need to establish as your normal grasp pressure.

You'll probably find that the resulting pressure is much greater than you would otherwise exert without doing this drill. It's the amount you need to apply every time you achieve your shooting grasp. Remember what that feels like and from now on, anytime you extend the gun to fire a shot, make sure that you are exerting that level of pressure. (I actually do this little routine at the start of each practice shooting session, just to remind myself how much grip pressure I really need.)

You'll also discover that, with occasional practice, your muscles will rapidly develop from this isometric exercise. The strength of your grasp will increase and you'll have increasing control over your pistol. You'll never get there, however, if you don't start now.

TRIGGER CONTROL

In my own experience, plus that of my students, learning how to operate the trigger properly pays more dividends than obsessing about sights or sight pictures. I can show you a drawing of a "proper" sight picture and you can grasp it immediately, but trigger control (particularly with DA and DAO guns) requires some good instruction and practice time.

The DA guns, in particular, require a significant amount of attention because you'll need to master two very different triggers: the heavy, long double action for the first shot and the much lighter single action for subsequent shots. Then you need to work to rapidly "change gears," so to speak, between them as you shoot a realistic string of fire.

Each of the trigger actions is slightly different, so let's look into those differences and how they affect your technique and training.

"Safe action" triggers

The "safe action" striker-fired pistol (as typified by Glock) generally has a trigger weight in the neighborhood of 7-8 lbs. It does have fairly short travel (at least compared to any of the double-action flavors) and most people can shoot very well with them.

I've found that putting the trigger in the crease of the first joint of the trigger finger gives me the leverage I need to easily overcome the weight of the trigger, an observation borne out by my student's experience. This is the old "power crease" that revolver shooters use, and it's ideal for dealing with the safe action triggers.

One of the issues commonly encountered with these actions is "steering" the gun – pulling it to one side as the finger comes back – and the cure for that is to pretend that your finger ends at that first joint. Pretend that you're pressing the trigger with the knuckle, not pulling it with the finger tip. That keeps you from curling the tip of the finger inward as you compress the trigger, which in turn greatly reduces steering.

Single action triggers

The single action trigger will usually measure in the 3-5 lb weight range and will have a travel that is far shorter than even the safe action guns. I've found that this short, light trigger benefits from a slight change in technique if it's to be manipulated both safely and efficiently.

I recommend that your finger be placed on the trigger not on the first joint, but in the middle of the pad of the finger. I've found putting the trigger closer to the crease of the finger joint, as we'd do with some other action types, results in too much leverage relative to the trigger weight. In my case I can't feel the very light trigger and this can result in an inadvertent shot being made. By putting the trigger on the pad, which is very sensitive, I can feel the trigger and how much pressure I'm applying.

Doing this makes it much easier to press the trigger straight back, and gives a tactile feel to the trigger stop, both of which reduce the "steering" effect mentioned earlier.

(Some will recommend that you center the trigger on the tip of the finger, but I've observed that position is hard to replicate exactly at speed or under induced stress; putting it in the middle up the pad, or up to the point where the edge of the trigger next to the crease of the joint, seems to be easier to replicate and doesn't result in any loss of control.)

Double-action only (DAO) triggers

A DAO pistol is the equivalent of a magazine-fed revolver; the long, heavy trigger is common to both, and the technique for mastering it is as well.

The trigger on a DAO pistol should be centered on the crease of the first joint of the finger. This is the point where you can generate maximum leverage to overcome the weight of the trigger, but still have enough reach and control to modulate your trigger press correctly. Many of the DAO guns I've tested come in with 8-9 lbs of pressure needed to operate the trigger, which necessitates a rock-solid grasp.

Now if you were to diagram the operation of both your trigger and your finger, you'd notice a similarity: both rotate around a pivot point, and both travel in a semicircular path. Neither travels in a straight line.

When operating a trigger, your finger hinges at both the proximal and distal interphalangeal joints, with most of the rotation happening at the latter. The tip of the finger therefore makes an arc (with a slightly decreasing radius, for the geometry purists in the audience) on a horizontal plane. The trigger pivots too, on a pin inside the frame, and the tip of the trigger also travels in an arc (this one is semicircular).

The arcs of the trigger and your finger are at a right angle to each other. This may not seem like much of a concern, but unless you understand what's happening you'll do the one thing that most people do to mess up their trigger stroke: you'll "hang onto" the trigger. That's because the trigger is traveling up and away from your finger, while your finger is traveling in toward your palm. The result is that the trigger always feels like it's trying to slip away from the finger, and the finger feels like it's going to fall off of the trigger.

When this happens most people strongly curve the tip of their finger inward in at attempt to hang on to the trigger. This action tends to pull the muzzle down and leads to steering the gun to one side – which side depending on how the gun fits the hand. (It's even worse when the tip of the trigger finger hits the frame of the gun just as the shot breaks, which it often does.)

Some people do that intentionally and try to "stage" the DA trigger – stopping to regroup near the point of ignition by using the tip of the trigger finger to contact the frame. Most people pause slightly, re-align their sights and then finish off the shot. In a defensive shooting situation there isn't time, nor fine tactile function, to allow this to happen. Don't allow yourself to stage the DA trigger!

I've got to admit that this can be difficult to overcome. I'm a fairly accomplished revolver shooter, and for a very long time I've trained myself not

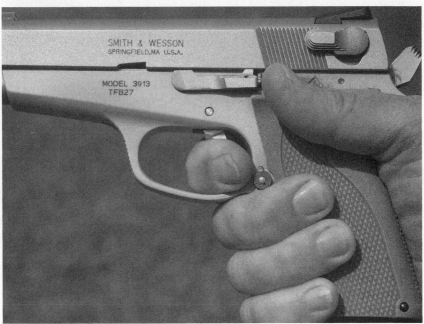

to "hang on" to the trigger with my trigger finger. Hand me the DAO Smith & Wesson 9mm that's sitting in my safe, though, and suddenly my finger is curling into the frame. Even I, with many uncounted thousands of rounds shot in double action, have to make myself think about NOT doing that on the pistol.

The key is very simple: let your finger slide on the trigger. It wants to anyhow. The finger wants to slide down and across the trigger face, and it's the reflexive resistance to that action – curling the tip of the finger – we want to avoid. Pay attention to how the finger feels on the trigger, and let it slide across the trigger face. It helps to think of your finger as ending at the joint, and paying attention to pressing the trigger with the joint, not pulling it backwards with the tip. Those two techniques, often used together, will help you get good hits from a DAO pistol.

It will still feel odd, but if you're like me you'll get the good hits that validate the technique.

Traditional double action triggers (DA/SA)

The DA guns have the same dynamics for the first shot as the DAO guns, so read above for the solutions; for subsequent shots, they have the same issues as the single action (SA) guns. The problem is switching between them.

The traditional double action has two distinct trigger types: long and heavy for the first shot, and short and light for subsequent shots.

There are several techniques espoused for dealing with the DA triggers. One says that you should place your finger in the same way you would place it if you were shooting exclusively SA, and accept the loss of precision on the first round that comes with the lack of leverage and control. The theory is that the rest of your shots can be made very precisely, which compensates for the poorer first shot. (Although I don't hear it much any more, there was a school of thought that said to fire the first shot as fast as possible, into the ground, so that you could shoot the gun "properly." Another idea was to thumb-cock the gun to SA on the draw, a seriously flawed technique on several counts.)

Another idea was to place the finger crease on the trigger for the first, heavy shot and then slide it slightly off, so the pad was on the trigger, for the rest of the rounds. While that might be feasible with a lot of work and training, I question whether it can be done when attacked – when tactile sensation and attention to minute techniques have both been affected.

Common issue is trying to "hang onto" the trigger as in first picture, curling finger and hitting frame. Letting finger stay relatively straight and slide on trigger keeps tip from curling in, makes manipulation easier.

I've found that the most efficient method is to keep the crease of the finger on the trigger for both DA and SA, paying particular attention to not involving the curling of the tip of the finger. That allows the best control of that first, heavy DA round and, with some practice, good control over the trigger for the lighter SA shots. Any curl of the finger will reduce control in the SA shots, so work diligently on the mental image of pressing with the knuckle, not pulling with the whole finger.

It's unlikely that the person who is the victim of the surprise criminal attack will even have time to cock the hammer.

Training that transition will require extra time, effort, and ammunition. It can be done, but it also requires frequent repetition to maintain the skills involved. This is one place where dry-fire comes in handy, because it will allow you to feel how the finger slides on the face of the trigger. It's not a lot of movement, mind you, but you should be able to feel that slight sliding effect. If you can, it means that you're doing it right.

Which brings me to a topic that is unique to the DA/SA pistol: the desire to cock the gun.

I suggest to you that the only way to become good with the DA pistol is to always shoot your first shot in double action, the way the gun comes out of the holster. This might seem ridiculously self-evident, but I've observed that people tend to take the easy way out when it's available. Shooting in double action is hard, and many people reach a point where they're not getting the hits they need in double action. They take the easy way out and either a) thumb-cock the gun for a nice, light single action release, or b) use the trigger primarily as a cocking device, all the while pretending the first bad shot didn't really happen and paying attention only to the remaining hits as indicative of their skill. Either case is counterproductive to mastering the double action pistol.

My argument is that you should never thumb-cock a pistol for any defensive shooting purpose, be it practice or an actual incident. Not only is the single action often very light, which is exactly the wrong thing you want in a

Never thumb-cock a defensive pistol!

trigger when you're trembling and your dexterity and tactile sensation have been reduced, it also has a very short travel to release. Cocking a pistol to single action during an actual attack is a bad idea simply because of the lack of control you'll be to apply to a very sensitive trigger.

It's also very unlikely that the person who is the victim of the surprise criminal attack will even have time to cock the hammer. The duration of these events, measured in a few seconds after the victim recognizes the need to shoot, leaves precious time for a measured, deliberate manipulation. The attacks happen very quickly, and the responsive shots will need to happen quickly as well. Most DA pistols don't have the big, easy-to-reach hammer spurs that are common on revolvers, and thumbing the hammer back (especially one-handed) is an awkward move with the very real risk of dropping the gun.

In later chapters we'll get into the need to practice realistically relative to the expected use, and part of that is using the gun in the same manner you'd expect to when it's "for real." That means double action for the first shot and then transitioning to single action. If you have a traditional double action pistol, it's going to be up to you to discipline yourself.

"RIDING THE RESET"

A currently popular shooting technique is variously known as "riding the reset" or "catching the link." It's a technique that came out of the competition world and was adopted by many in the "tactical" and defensive shooting communities.

The idea is to shorten split times (the time between shots) when firing a rapid string. Once the trigger is pressed and the shot fired, the trigger is released only to the point that it resets and is ready for the next shot – which can be half of the distance of its full travel.

There is a lot of debate about this even in competition circles, as some of the most renowned shooters use the technique and some don't. In the defensive shooting world it's become an "in-group" discussion point, where those who don't know about or don't use the technique are deemed to be somehow "lesser." I've actually heard people use that as an evaluation for who and who wasn't "serious about their shooting."

For defensive shooting I'm not a fan of the practice, for a couple of reasons. First, given the loss of manual dexterity and tactile sensitivity that occurs as a result of the body's reaction to a threat, I'm not convinced that I'll be able to feel the reset properly; this could lead to short-stroking the trigger which eats up far more time than just letting the trigger reset completely. Second, I don't believe the small gain in split time (measured in hundredths of a second) offsets the training time required to master the technique or the risk of short-stroking a trigger during an incident.

As a competition technique, where those hundredths of a second might count? Certainly. As a defensive shooting technique, where the conditions under which you'll shoot make those gains either illusory or risky? No.

I don't worry about trigger reset; I let the trigger return completely then start a new trigger press with each shot. It's more consistent, and I believe more repeatable under our natural threat reactions.

SOME THOUGHTS ON DRY FIRE PRACTICE

Practicing a smooth trigger press is quite difficult with live ammunition; the recoil of the gun masks movement of the sights (and the "feel" needed when first learning the double actions). That recoil also interferes with your ability to judge if you're correctly maintaining your grasp pressure.

Dry firing allows you to divorce the act from the recoil and lets you feel what a proper trigger is really like. Dry fire also makes it easy to feel grasp strength and if you're maintaining it consistently. Paying close attention to these things in dry fire will make a huge difference in live fire control.

While some may scoff at this, I'm generally not an advocate of extensive dry fire practice for defensive shooting. That isn't to say that it's completely useless, though, because some – of the right kind and in the right proportion – can be extremely helpful in developing proper trigger control.

I recommend doing just enough dry fire practice at home that you develop the ability to maintain a perfect sight alignment for the full stroke (press and return) of the trigger 100% of the time. Once you've achieved that, I maintain that further dry fire in isolation is of little value. That doesn't mean dry fire is completely useless, only that it might be best done at a different time and place.

In my experience, I found that once I actually fixed in my mind what proper trigger control felt like, any further dry firing was better done at the range just before live fire. This immediate transition from the lessons of dry fire to the application of those lessons in live fire provides far more benefit than endlessly dry firing off the range.

I suggest that when you go to the range start by doing a few dry fire repetitions, perhaps a dozen or so, which will be an immense help in fixing in your mind exactly what your hands should be doing. Immediately switching to live fire allows you to transfer the skills to actual shooting. My students have often reported that doing so makes both their dry fire and live fire sessions much more productive.

CHAPTER 15

EYES AND SIGHTS –

THE DEFENSIVE SIGHTING CONTINUUM

Shooting against another competitor is not the same as dealing with a predatory attack!

Missing from the last half-century of defensive shooting education has been an understanding of how our visual systems work, particularly when in a threat response. This has lead to defensive shooting students expecting to be able to do things they are unlikely to when actually facing a lethal attack.

Much of this has centered around the idea that because such things work in competition, mano-a-mano, then they must work in a fight, which is also mano-a-mano. Perhaps this is true in the kind of altercation where the violence is mutual (or at least anticipated), but the body's natural reactions make this highly unlikely when faced with the kind of sudden, one-sided threat that activates them.

CHANGES IN THE VISUAL SYSTEM

In the chapter on the body's natural reactions I touched on the changes to the eye: an increase in resolution in the center of vision and a corresponding increase in image detail to the visual cortex. The "why" should be obvious: to better see our threat.

Humans are visual creatures, and especially so when we're dealing with something that wants to harm us. Even in those cases where we achieve our initial startle reaction as a result of an audio stimulus, it's our vision that gives us the information about what the threat is doing which allows us to protect ourselves.

It's normal for the vision to focus on the threat when surprised by an attack. Your technique should take this into account.

That's not the only thing that our bodies do to help us out. Along with increase in resolution comes a locking of visual focus on the threat. The eye locks its focus at optical infinity, which is roughly six meters, and becomes less able (or completely unable) to change focus at will.(23) This combination of focus and resolution serves to fixate attention on the threat – which is exactly where we want and need it to be.

Given these very real physical changes, how reasonable is it to expect that you'll be able to focus precisely on a one-eighth-inch-wide piece of metal being held at arm's length? I'd say not very.

How then should you practice in anticipation of the changes in your visual systems? By using your eyes the way they've evolved to function: focused firmly on the threat.

START BY FOCUSING ON THE THREAT, NOT ON YOUR SIGHTS

Your visual system wants to focus on the threat to gather all the information it can to help you survive. Let it! Focus on the threat – in practice or training, your target – and simply bring the gun into and parallel to your line of sight.

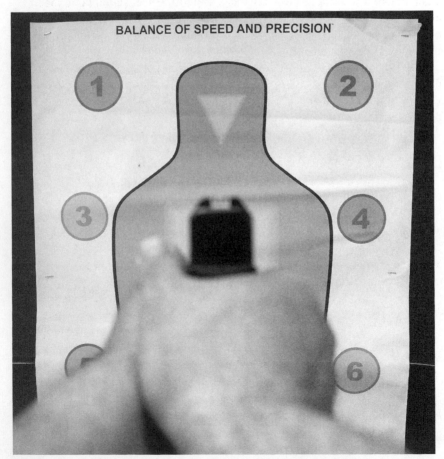

Start by focusing on the target, then simply bring the gun into and parallel with your line of sight.

Just because you're not using the little pieces of metal on top of the pistol doesn't mean you're not solidly indexing on target.

Most people, at the most likely defensive shooting distances, will have no problem getting high-center-chest hits, reliably and at speed, by simply doing this. Again: focus on the target, keep focused on the target, and as you do that simply extend the gun into and parallel with your line of sight. When the gun reaches full extension, press the trigger smoothly and swiftly. Make sure that you're using a natural, neutral stance, that you have equal extension with both arms, and that you have the strong, "crush" grasp I covered earlier.

By doing this you're using two methods of aligning the gun on target simultaneously: kinesthetic alignment, where you're physically orienting the gun onto the target, along with a non-cognitive visual component that encourages you to do things that are nice and symmetrical, in other words, parallel.

Orient to the target, focus on it, and bring the gun into and parallel to your line of sight. It's not hard, and it works – even people who have never fired a gun before can easily get vital zone hits, at 12 to 15 feet and in rapid fire, after less than a minute of instruction. I've done it with students and I've seen others do it with theirs. This technique is intuitive, because it works well with what the body does naturally.

This is most assuredly not "point shooting," in the sense that most people use that word. The gun is being indexed by the natural interaction of your visual line of sight and the mechanical alignment that your equally extended arms provide. Just because you're not using the little pieces of metal on top of the pistol doesn't mean you're not solidly indexing on target.

EXTENDING YOUR REACH

How far can you shoot effectively with this technique? It varies from person to person; you'll be different than me, and you won't know until you try. You need to train at varying distances, with varying sized targets, to find out what your limits are. In principle, however, as the precision required increases you'll need to apply more control over the deviation of your muzzle: you'll need to hold the gun steadier, slow down, and pay more attention to a smooth trigger press.

There comes a point, however, when the maximum amount of deviation control you're able to apply isn't sufficient to do the job without increasing the precision of your alignment. As it happens, your gun has precision tools built in that allow you to do this – they're called sights.

A sight is nothing more than an alignment guide. There's nothing magical about the sights on your pistol; they just help you align the gun on target. If you're a woodworker or a mechanic, you know all about alignment guides. They serve as handy references to help you put things together more precisely than you could by "eyeballing." Sights do the same thing.

I say this not to be overly simplistic, but rather to put you in the right frame of mind. For too long handgun sighting has been taught as an arcane

Sights exist to help you more precisely align the muzzle on target. They're alignment guides in the truest sense of the word.

art, one that you mastered only after learning the proper mantra and doing lots of gun kata. Get that out of your head: they're nothing but alignment guides, and they have a range of use from coarse to fine.

Once you've found the limits of your ability to align the gun on target by simply bringing it into and parallel with your line of sight, it's time to bring those alignment guides into play. Just as before, you're going to use that natural stance, keep your focus on the target, and extend the gun into and parallel with your line of sight. This time, though, you're going to take notice of your sights.

BALANCE OF SPEED AND PRECISION

Intuitive use of the sights: focus on the target and superimpose the sights. Look THROUGH the sights, not AT the sights.

Note that I didn't say "focus on your sights" – I said, and meant, take notice of them. Your focus will remain locked on the target, just as the clinical and empirical evidence suggests it will be – but you'll be deliberately aligning your front and rear sight onto the target. You'll simply superimpose the front and rear sights over your razor-sharp target. You're looking through the sights, not at the sights.

Your sights will be blurry and the target will be sharp. Don't worry, the alignment guides will still align, and with far better results than the traditionalists will ever acknowledge.

SIGHT ALIGNMENT

Let's take a moment to review how to use those alignment guides we call sights.

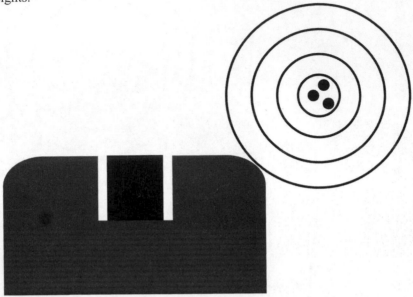

Unless you've done something absolutely wild with your pistol's sights, you'll have some sort of a blade at the muzzle and some sort of a notch at the rear of the frame. Using them is simple: put the blade inside the notch, with the tops level and an equal amount of light on either side:

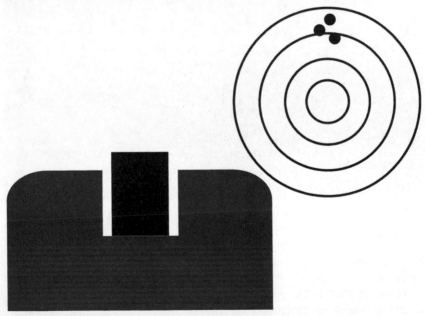

If the blade isn't level, you'll shoot high:

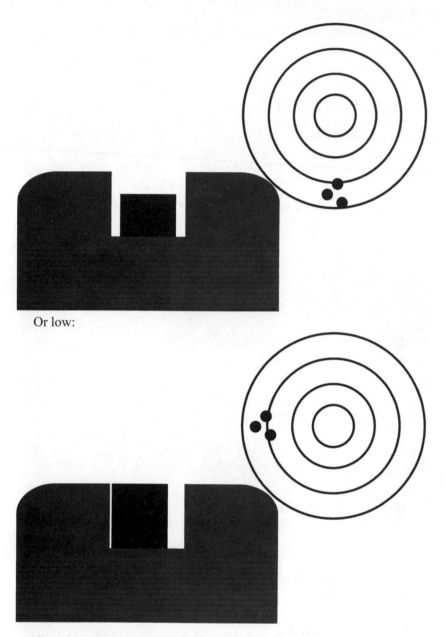

Or low:

If you have more light on one side of the notch than the other, you'll shoot to the opposite side:

Normally, the bullet will hit at the top edge of the front blade. If it doesn't, adjust your sights or change your ammunition – the middle of an attack is not the time to try to remember if your gun shoots high or low.

Proper sight picture

So, what does this focus-on-the-target sight picture look like? The target is sharp, the sights are slightly blurry – but aligned. That's the key. Focus on the target, align the sights, superimpose them on the target where you want to hit, and press the trigger smoothly, straight back.

Wailing and gnashing of teeth

The traditional method is to focus sharply on the front sight, align it with the rear, and superimpose the sharp sight picture onto the target. I don't deny that this is the best way to get highly accurate results, as long as a) you can in fact focus on the front sight and b) the target is of sufficient contrast to make the superimposition accurate.

As I've already mentioned when talking about the body's natural reactions, what science tells us in regard to our eye's performance under a threat reaction makes it more difficult to focus on that front sight. There are also those people (like me) who can't focus on the sights at all without prescription glasses, a problem which is likely to be worse – not better – when attacked! If you're one of those people who wears multi-correction prescriptions, you'll probably be physically prevented from focusing on your sights even if your body would allow it.

In addition, low contrast between the sights and target can make the super-imposition error greater than it would be by focusing on the target.

If you have the eyesight, it's occasionally helpful to practice with a traditional front sight focus to remind yourself what a good sight alignment looks like. My firm belief, however, is that the majority of your actual defensive shooting practice should be done with a target focus, with or without the addition of the alignment guides we call sights.

SO, WHEN DO YOU USE YOUR SIGHTS?

Simple: whenever you need to. Note that I didn't say whenever you can, but when you need to. It may not seem like much of a distinction, but it is.

Unless I were to do something extremely choreographed and unrealistic, there's really no training drill that I could give you where you couldn't use your sights. On the training range you've got full control of your responses, capabilities and faculties – nothing is interfering with your eyesight, no one is shooting at you. Under those conditions it's almost impossible to not use the sights.

During an attack, however, the body's natural reactions cause the eye to lose much of its accommodation – the changing of curvature to focus at different distances. The eyes tend to lock their focus on the threat in order to better see what's coming, which makes it much less sure that you'll be able to focus on that narrow piece of metal at the end of your arm. If you can't do that, you can't use those sights as traditionally taught. There is, therefore, a gap of ability between what you can do in practice and what you are likely to be able to do when attacked.

Training to use your sights whenever you can – which on the training range is "always" – and then getting yourself into a situation where you can't is a prescription for inferior performance. Instead, I suggest that you practice to use your sights only when you need to: when you need the additional precision that the alignment guides on the top of your pistol give you. If you're getting the hits you need to get without them, there's no reason to be expending the time (and effort) needed to use the sights.

Sights and efficiency

Remember that your goal is to be efficient. Using the sights in any manner will take a little more time than not using them. If you're spending that time using the sights when you don't need to, that time is wasted – you are being inefficient. Not using your sights when you need to means inaccurate shots, which is also inefficient. Using your sights when you need to is the most efficient method.

In practice, "whenever you need to" means whenever you recognize (see the expert concept coming in again?) that you can't achieve the level of precision dictated by the target without them. This means, again, that you'll need to train with various target sizes at various distances, preferably called at random by a training partner, and default to not using the sights until you reach failure. When you can't achieve the precision you need with the default, then you bring your sights into play.

Practice to failure, then change something to fix the failure. That's the only way you'll really learn when you need to use your sights (or anything else in defensive shooting).

THE MYTH OF EYE DOMINANCE

A staple of defensive shooting courses is the test to determine your dominant eye, then a prescription of what to do if – like many people – your dominant eye and dominant hand don't match. Usually this test involves some variation of focusing on a distant object, framing that object with your hands, and bringing your hands to your face while keeping the object in clear view. The eye over which your hands land is your dominant eye.

It's common, it's misunderstood, and it's irrelevant to defensive shooting.

A bit of knowledge goes a long way. You have a dominant eye only because your brain has become accustomed to using one eye, the dominant one,

If you've ever done this in class, it may be a sign that you weren't training in realistic defensive shooting skills.

for precise X-Y positioning and your other, subordinate, eye for z-axis (depth) information.24,25,26 This preference doesn't appear to be a function of physiology; it's just habituation, and as such it's possible to retrain your brain to make the other eye dominant, then switch back (I've done it myself).

The use of the eyes in a dominant/subordinate manner is how we see everything, how we gather all our visual information, and – most importantly – how we use tools. Our brain expects to see X-Y-Z information, and it puts that information together to form a three-dimensional image. Evolution has produced a visual system of tremendous ability that has facilitated not just our survival, but our progression as a species. Without it, man would not be a tool-using animal (and we would not be at the top of the food chain).

THE GUN IS A TOOL, AND THE BRAIN EXPECTS TO BE ABLE TO USE IT LIKE ANY OTHER TOOL

When you use a hammer, do you focus on the hammer head and let the nail go blurry? How about putting a key in a lock – do you focus on the tip of the key as you bring it to the keyhole? The answer in both cases is "no"; you'd find it insanely difficult to hang a picture or open your front door if you did!

We use tools (this is going to sound very familiar) by focusing on the endpoint of the task, putting it in the middle of our line of sight, and bringing the tool to the work. This is how we've evolved to use tools. That is how our vision works naturally.

When under the full force of a body alarm reaction, your visual system is unlikely to operate counter to the many thousands of years that has produced it. It is going to work as it always does, only now it won't be nearly as easy to voluntarily change it the way you can when practicing at the range. The body's natural reactions that occur as a result of the threat response ensure that the eyes work the way they've always worked – the way they want to work, the way they've evolved to work.

YOUR EYES AND YOUR SHOOTING STANCE

Being intuitive means using the tools of defense, your pistol, the way that your body works naturally: in this case, by focusing on the target. It also means bringing the gun into the center of your field of view and parallel with it.

If you adopt a shooting stance in training that brings the gun off-center, your visual system no longer works naturally. Instead of the gun being in the center of your field of vision where your eyes can work together naturally, the gun ends up in front of one eye. The brain can no longer put together the X-Y and Z-axis information, and one eye produces a picture that the brain can't integrate properly. If the dominant eye is not behind the gun, you won't be able to properly align the sights on target unless you close it (or do something else completely non-natural, like craning your neck at a severe angle to compensate).

These off-center stances are non-intuitive because they don't work with your body's natural reaction of squaring to the threat, nor your body's natural use of dominant and subordinate binocular eyesight. Focusing on the target,

Once-popular blade/bent elbows stances bring the gun out of optical alignment with both eyes and are non-intuitive by definition.

use of dominant and subordinate binocular eyesight. Focusing on the target, with a natural stance that puts the gun in the center of your field of view, is intuitive because it all works with how your visual system operates.

This is why the very tests that show you which is your dominant eye also show why it's unimportant: because you have to force your visual system to do something that it's not used to doing, something non-intuitive – which only proves that it doesn't work well that way.

This, I believe, goes a long way to explaining why, regardless of prior training or experience, we consistently see people on surveillance videos adopting the squared-off, neutral stance with both arms extended directly in front of their face. It's the way their bodies – including their visual systems – want to work. Why fight city hall when you don't need to?

---

[23]Paulev-Zubieta: "New Human Physiology", Ch. 6 (excerpted) http://www.zuniv.net/physiology/book/chapter6.html

[24]Pointer, JS: "Sighting versus sensory ocular dominance." J Optom. (2012), doi:10.1016/j.optom.2012.03.001

[25]Kromeier, M. et al.: "Ocular prevalence and stereoacuity", Ophthal. Physiol. Opt. 2006 26: 50–56

[26]Ehrenstein. W.H. et al.: "Eye preference within the context of binocular functions", Graefe's Arch Clin Exp Ophthalmol (2005) 243: 926–932

CHAPTER 16

DRAWING THE PISTOL

Most people think of the draw stroke in terms of getting the pistol into action as quickly as physically possible. There are trainers who have said that the first person to get his gun out of the holster is the winner. Many people spend inordinate amounts of time working to perfect the draw, to shave tenths of a second in order to beat a shot timer.

To a large extent this focus on sheer speed of the draw is an artifact of an overly competition-based approach to defensive shooting. The draw is some-

Just because something can be measured doesn't mean it's important to measure.

thing that can be timed, is too often timed, and thus commands more attention than may be appropriate.

As I said in an earlier chapter, very often in videos of actual attacks it's not drawing the gun that appears to waste the most amount of time – it's the decision making that leads up to the initiation of the draw.

None of the foregoing should be construed to mean that you should bring the gun out of the holster leisurely; quite the opposite. It's only that the draw needs to be kept in perspective given all of the other things that factor into your response.

REMEMBER CONSISTENCY?

The draw stroke should be consistent with all of your other gun handling skills. Remember when I said that consistency is a big part of efficiency? The draw stroke is a good example.

The physical part of the draw begins with getting a solid, firm grasp on the pistol. If you have covering garments, sweep them out of the way to allow your hand to grab the grip of the gun without getting anything caught.

There are a number of techniques suggested to move clothing out of the way, but I'm not going to ask you to over-think it. Simply figure out how to get your hand to the gun without grabbing any clothing along the way, and do that. Use your other hand, if necessary, to help you get the garments out of the way. Think not in terms of what to do with the clothing, but simply how to get your hand to the gun. I've found that students figure this out much faster without me introducing convoluted, choreographed maneuvers. (After all, when was the last time you needed to think about how to get through your covering garments to get your wallet out of your back pocket?)

Once you have a solid grasp on the gun, defeat any retention mechanisms that your holster might have. I'm personally not a big fan of retention holsters for a concealed pistol, but if you are that's fine; just be sure to practice smoothly unlatching or unsnapping or un-whatevering the thing as part of your draw.

Once you have that grasp, lift the gun straight out of the holster, parallel to your body so that you are not pointing it at any part of yourself. Bring it as far out of the holster as is comfortable; you don't need to do tendon damage to your elbow, just bring it as far out of the holster as you are able to do comfortably.

At this point orient the gun – point the muzzle – directly toward the target. You'll notice that you're now in a position that's very close (if not identical to) the high compressed ready position described earlier.

Here's where consistency comes in. If you've been practicing your grasp and extension, you're already accustomed to presenting the gun from this position. Your draw stroke is now automatically integrated with that part of your practice, and you'll see in the chapter on dealing with multiple threats that this integration will become useful.

Once your pistol is oriented on target, simply extend it into and parallel with your line of sight. You're ready to shoot, or to take the additional time and effort to use your sights.

Practice this in discrete steps first, then make it one continuous movement. Slowly at first, concentrating on where the gun is going; you'll find that you speed up naturally as you get used to the movements. Don't try to go faster until you can do it without error, without fumbling, and without pointing your muzzle at your own body.

INTEGRATION

This consistency in presentation keeps you from making a draw that interferes with your ability to get the gun oriented on target. If you come out of the holster and make a bee-line to the target, you're back to the problems we talked about earlier: the gun is coming up into your field of view at the same time you're reaching extension, which forces you to track the gun visually and stop its upward movement – then correct the inevitable over-shot to bring the gun back into alignment with the target.

If instead you practice the draw stroke as a logical development of the extension, you'll come out of the holster into the high compressed ready, then extend on the target – all in one fluid movement that automatically puts the pistol in a line that is parallel with your line of sight. The gun is already aligned on target, and all you have to do is reach extension; the alignment you'll need is already there and waiting for the trigger stroke.

The key is to draw the gun **through** the high compressed ready and extend on the target.

FREE TIME TO DISTRACT YOUR ATTACKER

The draw stroke takes time. Not a lot of it, of course, but it's time that you could be multi-tasking in a way that would keep you safer.

If your attacker is facing you and you move very rapidly to one side or the other, he'll need to shift his gaze to track you. Human tracking of rapid movement is very complex, but revolves around the brain trying to keep the target centered on the fovea.[27] If the movement is rapid and of sufficient angular distance, the brain has to first catch up then stop itself from over-correction.[28] This all takes time, and if the target stops suddenly it causes disruption in the brain's ability to predict where the target actually is going to be.

As you start to draw the pistol move laterally (sidewise relati to the threat) at least one full body width – very rapidly!

It's not a lot of time nor a lot of disruption, mind you, but it does happen and you can take advantage of it to help affect your attacker's ability to present a lethal threat to you. As you initiate your draw, simply take a large step at right angles (perpendicular) to your target and move at least one body-width to one side. Make the movement very rapidly, and if you can move more than one body-width in one step, so much the better.

Your attacker's brain has to react to your sudden, unanticipated movement, figure out where you're going, direct his eyes to catch up to you, and then react all over again when you stop suddenly. That's activity during which he can't as easily be hurting you.

Again, it's not a lot of time – but in your case it's free! You're already using that bit of time to draw your pistol, and if you can learn to move at the same time you're drawing this movement ends up costing you nothing.

Do not be mistaken: this motion is not going to magically keep your attacker from shooting or stabbing you, but it's going to make doing so a little harder. Looked at in financial terms, you've made a small profit without spending a cent.

When you practice drawing your pistol, move rapidly off the line of attack as soon as you initiate your draw stroke. Make sure that the movement is very sudden, that it's at right angles relative to the target, and that it's at least one full body-width – more if possible.

Some trainers call this "getting off the X," which is just a memorable way of saying "lateral movement." You should integrate lateral movement with your draw stroke every time you're on the range practicing or training. It costs you nothing and will help reduce your attacker's ability to mount a credible threat to you. Remember the old adage: free is a very good price!

SPECIAL CASES

When dealing with a draw stroke where the gun is other than on the hip, it's useful to go back and pay attention to the concepts: draw with the boreline parallel to your body so that you're not pointing the pistol at yourself, and orient the muzzle directly toward the threat.

Appendix carry is a good example. Appendix carry, which is where the gun is inside your waistband between your navel and hip, is getting very popular. It's quite fast to access and is very concealable (if one's wardrobe allows it).

As the pistol comes out of the holster keep it pointed straight down and parallel to your abdomen. This requires you to bend your wrist rather severely. Now rotate the gun directly toward the target: if you're a right-hander, this means rotating your wrist and forearm counter-clockwise. The pistol will now be on its side with the muzzle pointing at the target; simply extend as you bring the gun into and parallel with your line of sight. As you do so, your wrist and forearm will now rotate clockwise back into a normal shooting position.

The general procedure is the same if you choose to carry in a cross-draw manner. Cross-draw is really nothing more than appendix carry on the weak side, and the same concepts apply.

When considering pocket carry, drawing from a pocket isn't all that different from drawing from a belt holster. As you reach into your pocket make your rapid lateral movement. This will usually result in your leg being at an angle to your body, and the tendency is to draw the gun out and orient it vertically as you clear the pocket. If you do so, the muzzle will be pointed toward your leg! Remember: keep the gun parallel to your body. This means keeping the gun at the same angle as your leg until you get it oriented on the target.

I find that moving toward the side on which your gun is pocketed tends to result in a less severe angle and an easier draw as a result, but you need to practice moving to either side. Get used to thinking about keeping the gun parallel to your body until it has become a habit.

Bringing the gun up out of the holster from an appendix position. Note barrel is parallel to the body for safety and shooter is careful not to bring the muzzle higher than the hand that is pulling the covering garment away. (Holster courtesy of Crossbreed Holsters.)

THE COMPLETE MOVEMENT

At the moment you decide to draw, your body's natural reactions are all but certain to have been activated. You've had a flinch response where your hands have started moving toward your head, you've oriented (physically as well as visually/mentally/emotionally) toward your target, and your center of gravity

Once the gun is out of the appendix carry, orient the muzzle to the threat. Note that the gun is on its side, but the muzzle is on target.

As the arm extends, wrist rotates to bring pistol into upright shooting position.

has dropped to put you into something resembling a shallow crouch. Those are the circumstances under which your draw stroke will need to happen.

If that's the case, how much sense does it make to practice drawing your pistol while standing straight up? Unless you've got some warning about the impending attack (in which case why are you still there?), you're quite unlikely to be standing perfectly erect while you drawing your gun. Instead you should be training under the conditions you are likely to be when you're attacked: hands somewhere between your waist and your head, knees bent, body weight forward, squared off to the threat.

When drawing from a pocket, pay attention to the angle of your leg when the gun comes out; make sure barrel is parallel to leg and not pointing at your foot.

This is part of realistic training. Training and practicing your techniques under circumstances that aren't like what you're likely to experience only makes your actual response less sure, less efficient. Realistic training in this case means drawing your gun in as close to an approximation of your actual position as possible. Bottom line: if you're standing upright when you draw your pistol, you're probably not training realistically!

HOLSTER CHOICE AS A FUNCTION OF YOUR NATURAL REACTIONS

Whether from natural reactions or your trained responses, you should assume an aggressive, forward-leaning posture even before starting to draw your gun. As I've mentioned, if you're serious about training realistically you'll adopt that posture during all of your practice exercises.

If your holster choice is one of the belt-carry types, positioned anywhere other than your appendix, that natural position is going to affect how you draw the pistol, and some holsters don't work well under those conditions.

Cant and the draw

This is because a gun carried on a belt tends to stay in the same place relative to the hips, regardless of the position of the upper body. The shoulders, which carry the arms, move somewhat independently relative to the hips.

The instinctive threat reaction posture we've been studying, with the lowered center of gravity and the upper body lean, moves the butt of the pistol

Practicing a realistic draw means doing so from a lowered center of gravity, as you would when actually attacked.

This is not a position in which you're likely to find yourself when surprised by an attacker. Why practice this way?

backward relative to the arms. Because the shoulders are forward relative to the holster, you'll have to actually pull backwards to get the gun out of the holster. That's not the direction in which your arm is used to operating, nor where it has the most strength. There's also an emotional factor, brought about by the fear response: we tend to want to move the tool toward the threat, not away from it.

If you pick a straight-drop holster, that is one without a forward tilt, it will be less efficient and less intuitive to draw smoothly from this threat response posture. You can certainly make it work on a nice, threat-free range, but what about when your life is really on the line?

In contrast, the forward canted holster – often referred to as the "FBI cant" – will release relatively easily from that forward-leaning position. It doesn't work as well when you're standing straight up, which makes it a design that's not in favor with competition shooters. Under the conditions in which it is likely to be needed, however, it is more intuitive and therefore more efficient.

The canted holster puts the exit path of the gun into line with the position that the body is likely to find itself during an attack. It works better with both the body's natural reactions and your trained responses than the straight-drop holster design does.

Beyond the holster

Remember that I said your body's natural reactions affect how and what you train? It also affects what you train with. Any piece of hardware you choose to carry, whether it's a gun or a holster, needs to work well with what your body is going to do naturally.

The modern, striker-fired pistol fits the criteria very well because it needs no manipulation other than the trigger in order to shoot. It is an efficient design in terms of being able to react to a sudden threat. The forward-canted belt holster is in the same category.

Can you use a straight-drop holster for defensive encounters? People have certainly done so over the decades, but you now know that your hardware choice affects your efficiency. The more efficient your response, the less time that you'll be exposed to danger and the less chance you'll have of being injured – or worse – during the attack.

Don't allow yourself to be goaded into your holster selection based on what anyone else uses. If you understand your body's natural reactions, and understand the resulting lowered/leaning stance, you'll be able to make the proper choice.

---

[27]Findlay, John and Walker, Robin: "Human saccadic eye movements". Scholarpedia, 7(7):5095. http://www.scholarpedia.org/article/Human_saccadic_eye_movements
[28]Krauzlis RJ, Lisberger SG.: "Temporal properties of visual motion signals for the initiation of smooth pursuit eye movements in monkeys." J Neurophysiol. 1994 Jul;72(1):150–62.

CHAPTER 17

AFTER SHOOTING – ASSESS!

Y ou may have heard this before – it's common enough to be almost trite – but you live in a 360-degree world. If you're unlucky enough to need to shoot a criminal attacker, you're also going to need to deal with all the other things in your environment that may have an impact on your incident: bystanders, law enforcement, witnesses, other injured people, more threats, and so on. Here's how to do that.

STEP ONE: BREAK THE THREAT FIXATION AND CLEAR THE FIELD OF VIEW

I've been speaking of the body's natural threat fixation, which is a combination of the physical reactions and the emotional (fear) reactions to a lethal attack. The body tends to want to lock its vision and its attention on the threat in order to be able to react to it; to protect itself. Once you've shot and that threat has ceased (probably in the form of falling down), it's time to break that natural fixation and prepare to check your environment for anything important or relevant to your situation.

The first step is to get the gun out of your line of vision, which keeps it from blocking your field of view and removes it from your immediate attention.

After shooting, bring your gun back into that high, compressed ready position – clearing your field of view and helping to break the threat fixation.

Simply bring the gun back to the high compressed ready position you've been practicing. This brings it to a position you're accustomed to, one from which you can extend and engage if necessary (remember consistency). Make sure that you practice bringing your finger out of the triggerguard and placing it on the frame of the pistol as you come back to the ready, and activating the safety or decocker if your pistol is so equipped.

This clears your field of view so that you can actually look at your environment. Some trainers suggest that you simply swing the gun from side to side, or slightly lower it and do the same thing. The trouble with that advice is that the combination of the gun and your arms blocks anywhere from a third to more than half of your visual span. I would much rather be able to see as much of my environment as possible; if an accomplice is crouched down, waiting for his chance to attack, I don't want my gun or my arms to be in a position to block me from seeing him.

With the gun held at arms length, even if slightly lowered, you can't see the ground in front of you; you probably can't see your threat on the ground, where he may still be a threat; you won't see bystanders or witnesses cowering low; and you might not see the police officer crouched behind the water fountain ordering you to drop your gun (while you're pointing the thing at him!).

The commonly-taught lowered ready doesn't completely clear your field of view and is not consistent with any other technique you've learned here.

Bringing the gun back to the high compressed ready eliminates those problems. You now have a clear field of view, top to bottom and side to side, and you can examine your environment in detail without needing to point the gun everywhere you look.

STEP TWO: START SEARCHING

You need to do a visual search of your environment, an assessment, to find out if there is anything going on around you that might be pertinent to the incident. This means that you actually need to look at things and people in order to determine if they are in some way connected to your attack. An assessment is a search, and you can't do an effective search if your brain isn't engaged.

You're going to need to turn your head in order to survey your entire environment. Keep the muzzle of your pistol under control. I suggest that you keep it roughly pointed in the one direction you know it might be needed again: at your threat.

As you turn your head, make quick mental notes about what you're seeing, and mostly what you need to see are people. (You may decide to look for something to hide behind while you reload your gun, or simply to get out of the proximity of your threat. Doing the assessment thoroughly will help you

find that cover, but you need to actually see things. A quick spin of the head will only produce blurs.) This is why I say that the assessment is a search. A search means that you look for things, and that you actually see and think about what you're looking at.

Don't forget to turn to your other side and check what's over there, too!

STEP THREE: LOOK BEHIND YOU

Remember what I said about the 360-degree world? Now would be a good time to integrate that into your assessment.

You're going to need to look at the environment all around you, because you don't know where anything is going to be relative to your incident. Something very important, like Mr. Police Officer or another Mr. Bad Guy, could be directly behind you. You need to turn your head all the way around, from one side then the other, in order to truly see what's behind you.

Safely, of course

How do you keep your gun from pointing at things it shouldn't be pointed at while you're doing this? First, keep it roughly on the threat you've just engaged. Depending on your level of torso flexibility you may be able to do so by simply turning your head and shoulders all the way around to look behind you. If you don't have that flexibility (as I get older I find mine diminishing), it's okay to move your feet slightly to allow the shoulders to pivot as necessary.

If necessary, move your feet to allow a full 360-degree movement. Keep your muzzle under control; don't let it follow your eyes!

The assessment is a search – and you can't search if you're moving too fast to actually see anything.

Many trainers and schools teach a watered-down form of assessment, one where you simply wag your head from side to side; not only does it make the world go by too quickly for you to actually see anything, it also doesn't allow you to look at the whole picture. It's not realistic in any manner; don't do it! Look all around, and take the time to actually look at things.

PRACTICING THE ASSESSMENT

It can be a bit un-motivational to practice this on a range, where you don't have a lot of people (if any) or anything interesting to look at. Give yourself a challenge: look to see if anyone else has come in behind you; look to see if doors have opened or closed; check to see if the lights in the room next to the range have gone on or off; find out if any cars have come or gone; or even if birds have landed on the gravel. On any range there are things to look at, if you push yourself to do so.

If you're using a public shooting area out in the forest, say on Forest Service or BLM land as is common in the West, this may be both an exercise and a safety strategy. Many assaults have happened in such areas, and my own state has seen a couple of murders over the years by thugs who followed a hapless shooter into the woods with the intention of stealing his guns. In those environs the assessment is actually useful during practice, making it a two-for-one investment: you get needed practice and keep yourself safe at the same time.

HOW LONG SHOULD IT TAKE?

One of the questions that comes up in nearly every class I teach is "how much time should it take me to do an assessment?"

The answer is "I don't know."

The speed of the assessment, how rapidly and thoroughly you examine your environment, depends on the environment itself. If you're in the middle of a largely deserted parking lot with most people some distance away, your assessment is going to move a lot more rapidly than if you were in the middle of the mall with lots of people and furnishings around. If you have more to look at, it's going to take you longer to do the assessment. If you have fewer things to look at, it will take less time.

Assessment is a procedure, not an action; it has a purpose. If we tried to attach an arbitrary time for its completion it would no longer have a purpose other than to make the time. The assessment is a search, but a search with a defined purpose. Practice it thoroughly, and don't give into the temptation to make it a quick head wag or succumb to the notion that it must be completed on some sort of arbitrary schedule.

In a later chapter we'll talk about using the other half of the assessment process to deal with additional threats in your environment.

CHAPTER 18

DEALING WITH MULTIPLE AGGRESSORS

I n the chapter on assessment I mentioned that part of that process was the search for additional threats in your environment. As you look around and really see what's in your environment, one of the things you're going to be looking for is the presence of someone (or someones) who also intends to do you harm. You're looking for additional threats.

CURRENT EVENTS

While hard data is difficult to come by, the general consensus in the law enforcement community appears to be that attacks with multiple aggressors – such as home invasions, sexual assaults, and robberies – are on the rise. It's within the realm of plausibility that the attacker you shoot will not be alone and it might become necessary to find and, if the circumstances warrant, deal with another.

IT STARTS WITH ASSESSMENT

If multiple assailant crimes are on the rise, it's not hard to imagine that if you've had to shoot to stop a threat to your life there might be more than one attacker. This is why the first step in dealing with possible multiple threats is to do a thorough assessment: bring your pistol back to the high compressed ready, breaking your target fixation and clearing your field of vision to allow you to make a thorough search of your area.

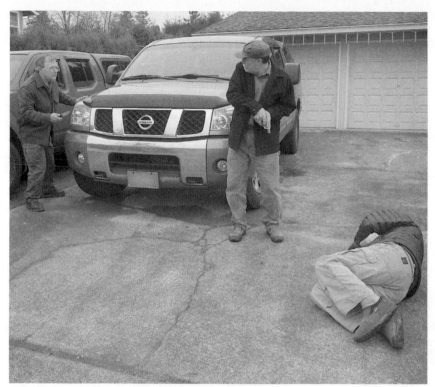
The assessment is the efficient way to locate – and deal with – any additional threats.

Remember that the assessment is a search, and you're searching for more people who pose an immediate, otherwise unavoidable threat to your life. This means that you actually have to look at the people in your environment. Does that person have a weapon? Is he/she acting in a manner that would lead a reasonable and prudent person to conclude that there was an immediate threat to your life? The only way you'll be able to ascertain this is if you actually look at the people around you.

Naturally, if someone is pointing a gun at you or if there are shots coming your direction the identification of that threat is probably going to be pretty easy. It might not, however, if all you've ever done is the head-wag scanning technique that's popular in some shooting schools. It also might not be easy if that person is crouched down behind some form of cover. That's why clearing your field of view to do the assessment, and then taking whatever time is necessary (no more but no less) to actually see what you're looking at is so vital.

As you turn your head from one side to the other to do your assessment, make sure that ayou remember to look at the threat you've already dealt with. He might be getting up to finish the job he started, or might have just enough fight left in him to pull a trigger. He's part of your environment too, and you already know that he's dangerous!

WHAT IF YOU FIND ANOTHER THREAT?

Let's say that you've been attacked, the threat is down, and while you're doing a thorough and diligent assessment you actually come across someone who poses a lethal threat. What do you do now?

Pretty much the same thing you did with the first threat: you forcefully move at least one body-width off the line of attack as you extend your pistol into and parallel to your line of sight and press the trigger smoothly until the threat ceases.

If that sounds familiar, that's because it is. What worked for the first threat – what was efficient – will also be efficient for the second threat. If there were something that was more efficient, you'd probably have used it the first time!

Body's natural reactions don't change either

Those learned, intuitive response don't need to change, largely because your body's natural reactions probably haven't changed. You'll still have the natural fixation on the threat, you'll orient toward the threat, your center of gravity will drop and your upper body will lean forward. Since you have a tool in your hand, your primitive grasp reflexes will likely cause you to grip it harder as you're surprised by the new threat; your shoulders may hunch a little as the combination of surprise and sudden grasp pressure tense those muscles.

Those things that worked well with what your body does naturally still work, because your body is doing the same things again.

WHAT DOESN'T MAKE SENSE

If you've taken some self-defense shooting courses you may notice that this method of assessment and response is somewhat different than the typical way that "multiple target" drills are done, especially in those schools that have a decidedly competition-based curriculum.

In most schools, training for multiple aggressors is done by lining up two or three targets and then practicing firing a certain number of shots at each one. As the students finish shooting the first target, they're taught to move their eyes to the next target as they swing the gun into alignment. This is called "transitioning," and is practiced so that the students get faster and faster at the drill.

The problem with this approach is that it only works if three criteria have been met: first, that the student knows ahead of time which targets are to be shot; second, that he knows where they are; and third, that they don't move relative to each other.

The problem in our world is that this just doesn't happen. You don't know ahead of time who needs to be shot, because criminals very often flank their victims; in a store, for instance, you might not even know there was an accomplice.

Even if you did have an inkling that there might be an accomplice, you wouldn't necessarily know where he was. Take a look at some surveillance camera footage from convenience stores; very often one thug comes in and

The swinging transition technique only works for targets like this.

goes directly to the counter, while the other hangs back and often goes down an aisle where he can keep an eye on things. You wouldn't know if he's to the right or left of the first attacker, and a large part of the speed advantage of the swinging transition technique is that you know in advance which direction you'll be looking.

Finally, even if you did know at the outset of the shooting who the accomplice was and where he was, it's a pretty good bet that he's not going to be standing still when rounds start going off. Even in the unlikely even that he was standing right next to the first threat you engaged, and he drew his gun at exactly the same time (and you knew that), by the time your gun gets out of the holster and you've engaged his buddy Number Two will have moved, out of a well-ingrained sense of self preservation if nothing else. You're going to have to look for him, which brings us back to where we started.

The swinging transition technique is based on the idea that you know exactly where you're going to look for the guy you've identified ahead of time, and that he's still there when you get around to him. I've yet to seen any solid evidence that this actually happens with real people committing real crimes.

AGAIN - FASTER DOES NOT MEAN MORE EFFICIENT!

You'll no doubt have people tell you that the swinging transition technique is faster. As I pointed out in the chapter on reloading techniques, faster is not the same as more efficient. In the context of a shooting game, the swinging transition technique is certainly more efficient because the very goal is to get to the next shot as fast as you can – and the environment is set up to allow just that to happen. Since the goal is faster, that technique is more efficient in that context.

In the context of a defensive shooting it's not as efficient because the conditions are counter to what makes it work in the first place. The targets are moving and thinking, two things that make any technique based on certainty fail, and you have those specific natural reactions that govern how you're going to be able to respond. The result is that you'll need to look for your next threat and when you find him, you have to deal with him. You have to **assess and respond**.

Sometimes this assess-and-respond cycle happens very quickly. You see the first threat go down from your shots, and just as you bring the gun into the high compressed ready and start your assessment you find the second threat. He might not be all that far away in real terms (especially in terms of angular distance – degrees), but you still had to locate him. Move laterally relative to him – remember, what was efficient for the first guy is still efficient for the second – as you extend and press the trigger.

If you go to a shooting match and start into an assess-and-respond cycle, I can guarantee two things are going to happen: you're going to lose the stage and everyone is going to laugh at you. The context for the assess-and-respond cycle fits the competitive environment no better than the swinging transition technique fits an actual defensive shooting. The context of use is different, and just because they both use a gun doesn't mean they're the same.

This illustrates why you need to train techniques that reflect both the reality of how attacks happen, and the reality of how you are likely to respond to them.

CHAPTER 19

RELOADING YOUR PISTOL IN AN EMERGENCY

This is going to sound contradictory, so read carefully: it's actually pretty uncommon to find instances where someone has needed to reload their pistol during an altercation. (It's more common in police service than in the private sector, but still not an everyday occurrence.) The reload process as a component of your response training, then, wouldn't seem to be terribly important. Yet, reloading the pistol in an emergency is a foundational skill, one that's important to understand and master.

If it's not needed very often, why would we consider it a foundational skill?

Several reasons: first, though the need to reload doesn't happen very often (low incidence), it's pretty important when it does happen (high consequence). Second, it's an integral part of the malfunction clearance process (another low incidence/high consequence skill); and finally, training the reload is "free" because you need to do it anyhow.

Put another way, when the need to reload during an incident occurs, it's probably because you still need to be shooting; the fact that you've already shot a number of rounds is an indication that your life is in grave danger, and getting they gun back into a firing condition is necessary to preserve your life.

If the gun stops firing for any other reason than being out of ammunition,

the reload is still a major part of a comprehensive malfunction response; it comes very early in the clearing process, and the end step of clearing a malfunction is getting the gun loaded again.

As it happens, practicing the skill of efficient reloading is also easy to work into a training regimen – because anytime you train or practice, you're going to run the gun empty many times, which gives you many chances to practice a proper reload. From the standpoint of efficient use of time and effort, training to reload your gun is actually "free" because you have to do it anyhow just to be able to shoot.

We'll delve more into malfunction clearing in the next chapter, but for now let's look at the reload as a separate skill.

ONE TECHNIQUE TO RULE THEM ALL?

Believe it or not, the simple act of reloading the gun is the source of a seemingly never-ending stream of articles and online arguments. Everyone, it seems, has his or her idea of what constitutes a "proper" reload technique and will defend their point of view with vitriol whenever questioned.

What you'll often find are specific reload techniques for all kinds of scenarios, some of them ridiculously specific. Even the name of any give reload procedure is open for conflict! Usually, however, most people break down reloading techniques into two broad categories: those where you need to reload, and those when you want to. The difference is whether or not you had the option to choose your response.

While there is some merit to that approach, I believe a simpler one makes better use of your scarce training resources: you should learn how to reload your gun when you need to, when the gun has run empty, because a) that's the situation where you really need a practiced skill, and b) it's the technique that's directly related to clearing malfunctions in your gun.

The so-called "tactical" reload, where you preemptively put a fresh magazine in the gun before the old one is depleted, doesn't address either of those points. It's something you can think about doing and choose to do, and therefore I contend doesn't really need the kind of skill development that the empty gun emergency reload does. I'm therefore going to suggest that you focus your time and energy on learning how to get the gun up and running again in the most efficient manner possible when it's forced upon you: the worst-case scenario.

A reload, as I define it, is done at slide lock: when the gun has run empty because you've fired all of the available ammunition, resulting (usually) in the slide being locked back on that empty magazine. It's the worst thing to have happen, and it's also more likely to occur during an attack than is having the luxury of deciding to reload. Because of its sudden and important nature it's worth spending the time to learn to do it efficiently.

WHAT DOES AN EFFICIENT RELOAD TECHNIQUE LOOK LIKE?

The reload, remember, is done because you've been forced to do it: you're under attack, you've fired all of the rounds in your magazine, and you find yourself holding an empty gun with a maniac still standing in front of you. (Okay, that's a bit hyperbolic I'll admit – but it does give you a picture of when and why you'd do one.)

You want to get the gun reloaded as quickly as you can, keeping in mind several things:
- You're still being attacked.
- You might want to be doing your best to avoid his blows or bullets while you get your gun back in action.
- Your motor skills are likely to be affected because of your body's natural reactions to his attack (more in a later chapter).
- You're likely to be fixated on the ongoing attack (again, a natural survival tactic).

- You're probably going to be scared out of your wits (I know I would be!).

Given all that, an "ideal" reload technique would probably:

- Rely as little as possible on fine motor skills.
- Work even when your attention is focused on your threat.
- Work under the widest range of environmental circumstances: in the dark, while it's raining, etc.
- Be just as easy to do while you're moving to avoid your attacker as when you're standing still.
- Be as fumble-proof as possible under the circumstances.
- Be as automated as possible to free your mind to deal with your attacker.

Here's how to do it.

1. Keep your focus on the threat: the fact that you need to reload your gun doesn't change the situation; the bad guy still wants to hurt you, and isn't going to stop and politely wait for you to get your gun running again. You might need to evade his attack, you might need to evade his buddy coming to help out, you might need to look for something to hide behind, but whatever the situation keeping track of what your attacker is doing is both natural and necessary. The best part is that you can learn to reload your pistol without the need to look at it.

2. When you recognize that your slide is locked back and out of ammunition, start to bring the pistol back into the high compressed ready position. This position is consistent with where we'll be doing lots of other tasks, such

as malfunction clearing; it's the position where our strength and dexterity are their greatest; and it's a protected position, which allows us to move easily should it be necessary during the reload.

3. As you start bringing the gun back, your support hand goes directly to the spare magazine (wherever that is).

4. At the same time your support hand is heading for the spare ammunition, and on the way back into the ready position, push the magazine release to drop the empty magazine from the gun. If you can't reach or operate the release from a firing grip, work your hand around the gun so that you can – but don't "flip" the gun, which is a complex act that requires pretty significant coordination. Move the hand around the gun, not the gun in the hand. Once the magazine is free, work your hand back into a firing grasp as you come into the ready position.

5. Bring the spare magazine out from wherever it's being carried. Keep it close to the body, and don't let it drop below the level of wherever your retrieved it.

6. Forcefully insert the magazine into the gun, using the heel of the palm to make sure that it's firmly seated.

7. Rotate the free hand up and over the top of the slide, grasp the slide firmly to trap it between your fingertips and palm, and pull back on the slide while you push forward with the gun's grip.

8. Immediately release the slide to chamber a round and re-establish your firing grasp.

9. MOVE! It's difficult to show in pictures where we're focusing on the steps of a procedure, but one of the important components of the reloading process is your movement. You're standing in front of a threat that you may or may not have neutralized; for the period of time it takes you to get the gun loaded again, you are unarmed. Your gun is impotent and incapable of helping you against that threat, or any others that might be in the vicinity. In that kind of a situation, how about doing something that will negatively affect his ability to harm you?

That something is movement – specifically, laterally with regard to the threat (perpendicular to a line between you and the threat, if you prefer to think of it that way). By moving laterally, very rapidly, as you reload you're negatively impacting your attacker's ability to mount a lethal threat, without markedly affecting your ability to get your gun reloaded. This is one of the reasons why you should learn to reload your gun close to your chest (where your strength, dexterity, and control are at their best), and to be able to look at something other than your gun while you get it recharged. Those two components of the reload allow you to evade your opponent and to make it harder (not impossible, you understand, just a bit more difficult) for him to hit, stab, or shoot you. Once your gun is operational again, you can stop moving.

When should you move? As soon as you recognize that you're out of ammunition (usually because your slide is locked back), you should start moving! Keep moving as you bring the gun back, drop the empty mag, retrieve and insert the new magazine, rack the slide, and come back to your firing grasp. If you need to shoot, stop moving!

I'm not talking about a slow slide-step or walk, either; move quickly and with purpose. In class I have my students running as they reload their guns (space and safety concerns permitting, of course). They're often surprised to find that they can efficiently reload a pistol without looking at it and while moving quickly. It's one more way to help you survive the attack.

SOME FREQUENTLY ASKED QUESTIONS ABOUT THE RELOAD

Why not use the slide stop to release the slide?

Remember when I said that reloading techniques were the source of arguments? Here's one example: racking the slide to chamber a round versus using the slide stop to release the slide and chamber a round.

One reason to do so is that hitting the slide stop is a dexterity-intensive task that is likely to be made more difficult by the body's natural threat reactions. Notice that I didn't say "impossible," only that it's going to be more difficult due to the decrease in tactile sensation, dexterity, and extremity strength. My goal is to make things simpler and easier whenever possible and if racking the slide does so, that's the most logical choice.

Another issue is consistency of technique. If for some reason the slide is already forward when you insert the new magazine, you don't have to use a different technique (nor does your mind need to do the conditional branching necessary to pick the right technique) to get the gun back into action. The technique doesn't change, which makes training and recall easier.

Hitting the slide stop is a dexterity-intensive task that is likely to be made more difficult by the body's natural threat reactions.

It's also consistent with the first part of a malfunction clearing sequence, making the response to any pistol stoppage (regardless of cause) more efficient.

My gun automatically releases the slide when I insert a magazine. Do I still need to rack the slide?

Yes. On occasion, forcefully seating a magazine will cause the slide stop to disengage and allow the slide to ride forward, usually (but not always) chambering a round in the process. This happens very often with modern polymer framed guns, like Glocks and the Smith & Wesson M&P, especially if they've been used extensively. On some guns the probably of this happening is close to 100%.

Many people count on this in their training, under the mistaken impression that it makes them faster. From our perspective as defensive shooters interested in overall efficiency, counting on that is not consistent with our goal.

First, a reload technique where the slide isn't racked to chamber the round deprives us of the opportunity to get in a malfunction remediation repetition. Remember that one of the big values in the rack-the-slide method is that it builds response skills for clearing other kinds of malfunctions, and it's the opportunity of repetition because reloading is so common that adds to the value. Taking that away by allowing the slide to run of its own accord denies us that valuable "rep."

Second, the gun doesn't always chamber a round when the slide runs forward! In some cases it's very reliable, but in my experience it's never 100%. Sooner or later the gun will fail to feed a new round and on pulling the trigger you'll get "click" instead of "BOOM." Now you have to perform a malfunction drill (which, remember, you have fewer reps of) to get the gun into the charged condition it should have been in the first place. Racking the slide every time brings the certainty of chambering close to perfect, and for those rare times when it's not you've got the response pattern of tap/rack in place.

Even if you're absolutely sure you can get your gun to auto-forward every time, rack the slide anyhow.

Should I carry my spare magazine with the bullets forward or backward?

Frankly, it really doesn't matter – at least, it doesn't matter as much as some people would have you believe.

There are two schools of thought on the matter of positioning the spare magazine on your person: bullets facing forward, so when the magazine is drawn your forefinger is on top of the bullet noses; or bullets facing back, so that when you grab the mag your thumb is on the primer side of the cartridges.

Over the last few decades competition shooters have come to favor the bullets forward position. This is largely because the insertion of the magazine into the pistol is slightly easier when the gun is in their preferred reloading position (up and in front of their face). Because of competition's influence on pistol shooting in general this has become the norm in the defensive shooting world – so much so that, if you show up to a range or a class with your bullets facing anywhere other than forward, people will often warn you that your magazines are "backward."

Having the bullets facing to the rear, however, has some advantages as well. First, it's easier to retrieve a spare magazine from a pocket or other confined carry space, as the hand doesn't twist sideways to put the forefinger to the front of the magazine. Second, the elbow doesn't stick out as much during retrieval, making reloading in close quarters or among other people a bit easier. Finally,

It's not necessary to look at your gun to reload it! Reloading can be done with the gun below the line of sight, allowing you to keep your vision where it belongs: on the threat.

it's more consistent with the way that most people end up handling magazines when reloading their semiautomatic rifles (if they have one, of course).

I started out with my bullets facing backward, simply because it felt more natural to me (and no one told me it was "wrong"). I quickly changed to the bullets forward position when I started competing, largely because that's how the pros did it. A few years ago I changed back to thumbs-on-primers, because that's how I handle my AR-15 and FAL rifle magazines and I want that consistency in technique. I'll admit that I still feel more confident doing it with bullets forward, since I did so for many years, but I find that there's actually very little performance difference between them.

What I recommend to my students on the range is the same thing I'll recommend to you: if you're already accustomed to bullets forward, just keep doing it that way. It's not worth the time and effort you're going to spend to correct that past training and practice. On the other hand, if you're new to pistol shooting I recommend that you train with bullets backward; I think you'll find that technique usable over a slightly wider range of circumstances, particularly in concealed carry and especially if you spend a lot of time shooting autoloading rifles.

PRACTICING THE RELOAD

It's tempting to practice your reloads to make them faster. Many in the business will prescribe such things as weighted dummy practice magazines, or real magazines loaded with Snap-Caps or weighted dummy rounds, to practice with. My experience doing this in a competition environment was not altogether successful: while I got really fast at the manipulation part, that didn't help everything else that went along with the need to reload my gun.

> *Recognition of slide lock – the indication to perform the learned skill of reloading the gun – is usually (and usually by far) the most inefficient part of the process.*

What I see with most students is that the recognition of slide lock – the indication to perform the learned skill of reloading the gun – is usually (and usually by far) the most inefficient part of the process. That brief period of time while they stop to analyze what happened and then decide to initiate that reload almost always exceeds the time they shaved on the manipulation portion by doing endless dry repetitions of the reload. It was certainly the case with me.

Dry practice omits that stimulus of achieving slide lock in a string of fire. In dry practice the slide is pre-locked to the rear; there is no stimulus of the slide dynamically locking itself to the rear, no change in recoil pattern because of the difference in weight distribution, and no sensation of the slide failing to return to battery. All of those things, taken together, are what tell us that our gun is out of ammunition and needs to be recharged. Without that, we have to spend time analyzing why the gun isn't running and then decide to initiate the reload. With that stimulus, we can use the brain's ability for recognition and recall to make that decision (and execute that decision) far more efficiently.

I'll recommend some dry practice simply to get used to the mechanics of the reload, particularly if the student is having trouble in that area, but beyond that I believe it's far more important to practice that skill in context, in the manner that you'll actually need to use it. That means shooting to experience slide lock and developing the ability to perform the reload in direct response to that stimulus, without cognitive thought. The only way to do that is to use live ammunition on a real range.

SLIDE FORWARD PRACTICE

Whether dry or live, you'll often see people practicing "reloading" by leaving the slide forward. This leads to much faster times because two things have been eliminated: the need to reload in response to a stimulus, and the need to manipulate the slide after seating the magazine. You've probably seen YouTube videos of people performing scarcely believable speed reloads, but with the slide forward they're not really reloads: they're just pre-determined topping off exercises.

In a defensive encounter, where you've been attacked and are forced to respond, the most dangerous point is when you've shot all your rounds and your slide is locked open: the empty gun. This is where you really need those reload skills, and you really need them to be practiced so that you know you're empty, you respond by reloading the pistol, and finish by chambering a new round so that you're ready to shoot again (if necessary).

Practicing with the slide forward in no way prepares you for that situation. You're choreographing an action, as opposed to performing a response to a

stimulus. Yes, it's very impressive and you can do many such "reloads" in a small amount of time, but they're indicative of nothing in regards to defensive shooting. Practice and perform your reloads in live fire when the slide locked back. Anything else is just a waste of your limited training time.

CHAPTER 20

MALFUNCTIONS – WHAT THEY ARE AND HOW TO DEAL WITH THEM

An autoloading pistol depends on a number of interacting forces in order to function properly. Of course the ammunition must be correct; the springs that absorb recoil and reset the pistol must be of the proper weight and strength; and the hand that holds it must supply enough stability that the forces aren't wasted in unnecessary motion.

When all that is considered, the engineering behind the modern semiautomatic pistol is impressive. On occasion, however, and for any number of reasons a pistol can fail during use. It's up to the shooter to correct the issue as quickly as possible.

DEALING WITH A MALFUNCTION DURING AN ATTACK

When your pistol stops running on a nice, calm shooting range, it's a relatively easy thing with which to deal. You can take the time and devote the energy to figure out what happened and choose a remedial action. That's in fact how a lot of malfunction responses are usually developed.

Imagine, though, that your pistol has stopped functioning while your attacker is in the process of trying to hurt you or your family; no matter how well you've trained, don't you think that your primary response is probably going to be sheer panic? Mine probably would be! At that point your best tool to deal with that malfunctioning pistol is a well-rehearsed sequential approach that doesn't require you to diagnose a problem and recall a solution. What we're looking for is an automated response that effectively deals with all of the likely malfunctions that can be rectified in the middle of an attack. In the Combat Focus® program, it's referred to as a "non-diagnostic linear malfunction drill," and that's a very good description.

"Non-diagnostic" means that you're not going to take your visual attention off of your threat while you try to figure out why your gun isn't working. Back in the old days we would drill malfunction clearing by first looking at the malfunction, classifying it (Type 1, 2, or 3), then applying the proper remedy. It took time, it took attention away from the threat, it required cognitive thought to implement, and it resulted in task fixation manifested in an inability to move to safety or evade a continuing attack.

Today we know that we can train an automated process that addresses the kinds of malfunctions that occur in a systematic way, without needing to fixate on the problem or try to figure out exactly what happened. This automation, done without cognitive attention, is made possible by the linear nature of the procedure.

"Linear" simply means that you go through the steps in order. At any given step, if the gun starts working, you stop and get back to your defense. If one step doesn't fix the problem, you go onto the next step without pause. The arrangement of the steps results in the most common malfunctions being fixed before those that are less common. By the time you get to the end of the process, if the gun still isn't working it's because something has happened that you can't fix in the moment; you need to implement whatever backup plan or tool that you have for just that sort of happenstance.

Let's look at the steps, in order, and look at the malfunctions each solves.

YOUR GUN HAS STOPPED SHOOTING! NOW WHAT?

Step 1: Keep your eyes up, on the threat or on your environment. This allows you to move to cover, to keep tabs on what your attacker is doing, or to simply move to reduce your attacker's ability to present a lethal threat to you. The non-diagnostic, linear nature of this malfunction procedure means that you don't need to look at your gun to get it running again.

Step 2: Bring the gun back into the high ready position, where your strength and dexterity are greatest. You don't need to bring it up in front of your face, and you don't want to be manipulating the gun held out in front of you where your strength is lessened. Bring it in close to your chest, at roughly the height of the base of your sternum, and do all of the manipulations there.

Step 3: TAP-RACK. Tap-rack (or T/R) simply means to hit the base of the magazine with the heel of your palm, seating it firmly, and then racking the slide to chamber a new round. Many times the magazine gets released from its catch but stays in the gun, or sometimes the magazine doesn't get seated firmly when it's loaded into the gun (particularly common when loading a full magazine into a pistol when the slide is forward, as when you "top up" with a full magazine). This causes the gun to fail to pick up a new round, and your first indication is the trigger going "click" but no shot fires. When that happens, the immediate response needs to be TAP-RACK, then go back to shooting (if you need to, of course). If the gun still fails to fire, you go immediately (linear, remember) to Step 4.

Now if you've simply shot the gun dry but failed to recognize slidelock (hey, it happens to the best of us), as soon as you reach up to RACK the slide after doing the TAP you'll feel that it has locked back on the empty magazine. If the magazine is empty but somehow failed to lock back (happens frequent-

ly with worn magazines), you'll feel the slide lock and fail to go forward as you rack. If either of those things happen the TAP-RACK will fail to solve the problem, and you need to go to Step 4.

Step 4: RELOAD. If the TAP-RACK failed to solve the problem, most of the time it means that the magazine is empty or permanently damaged and needs to be replaced. Perform a reload procedure, just like we discussed in the last chapter: drop the magazine, retrieve a new magazine, insert the fresh mag into the gun, and overhand rack the slide to chamber a new round. If the reload is successful – the old magazine dropped out, the new magazine went in, and the slide went forward when racked – you can get back to shooting as necessary.

There are situations where the reload can't be completed for some reason. Either the magazine won't drop free or, when the new magazine is inserted, the gun won't chamber a new round. These things usually happen with true

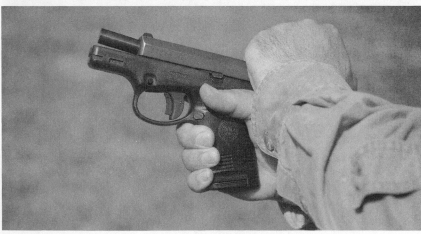

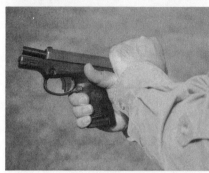 

"jams" – double feeds, failures to eject, or failures to feed. Whatever the issue, the gun can't be reloaded in the normal manner and it's time to go to the final step of the procedure: the complex reload.

Step 5: COMPLEX RELOAD. The first step in the complex reload is to get the old magazine out of the gun. Grab the base of the magazine, depress the magazine release, the RIP the magazine out of the gun. Some guns are easier to do this with than others; if you can't get a good grasp on the magazine, or you can't get the magazine free, pull the slide back, LOCK the slide open, and then RIP the magazine free.

Once the magazine is out of the gun, you need to CLEAR the gun of any obstructions (stuck cases or double-fed rounds) by racking the slide three times: RACK-RACK-RACK. Then retrieve a new magazine, insert it into the gun, and rack the slide to chamber a new round.

If at any point after you complete a reload you get a "click" when you pull the trigger, TAP-RACK.

PRACTICING THE MALFUNCTION DRILL

With most modern, properly maintained guns loaded with good quality ammunition, malfunctions are likely to be few and far between. However, the prospect of a non-functioning firearm when you need it most carries enough consequence that it's worth the time and effort to occasionally practice a malfunction drill.

First, any time you pull the trigger and get anything other than a "bang," you should immediately TAP-RACK. Get into the habit; the stimulus of

Complex reload: press up on slide stop lever to lock the slide open

Press the magazine release and rip the magazine out of the gun

Rack....

...rack...

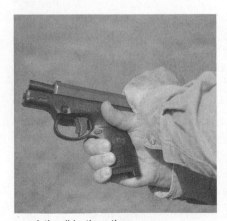

...rack the slide, three times

Reload and chamber a new round

"click" should result in an immediate recall and execution of the skill TAP-RACK. This can be an issue if you're a competitive shooter; the "unload and show clear" procedure at the end of a course of fire requires the shooter to pull the trigger on an empty chamber to prove the gun is empty. It's possible, in a day of shooting, to get more repetitions in "click-do nothing" than "click-TAP-RACK."

A good way to get some practice and help you link the stimulus (hearing the "click") with the execution of the skill (TAP-RACK) is to have a training partner slip a snap-cap or two into your magazines at random. When you hit the snap-cap the gun won't fire when the trigger is pulled, forcing you to do a TAP-RACK to clear the dummy round and chamber an actual round. (If you don't have a training partner, you can do it yourself – but put the dummy rounds in randomly, use several magazines, then shuffle the mags so that you don't know which ones have the dummy, let alone where in the magazine they are!)

This procedure doesn't help with any of the other kinds of malfunctions, however. To get practice with all of the kinds of malfunctions you're likely to experience, you'll need a few things: some pieces of expended brass from your gun, a few orange plastic Saf-T-Trainer dummy rounds, and three magazines. (You can do it with two magazines, but you'll find that you'll have to stop and refill them often.)

You'll need to prepare the Saf-T-Trainer rounds by taking a nail clipper and clipping off a piece of the rim in two places. The placement of the missing pieces isn't critical, but do it twice to each round.

Now, take your expended brass and your modified Saf-T-Trainers and randomly put them into your magazines along with the live ammunition. (Bet-

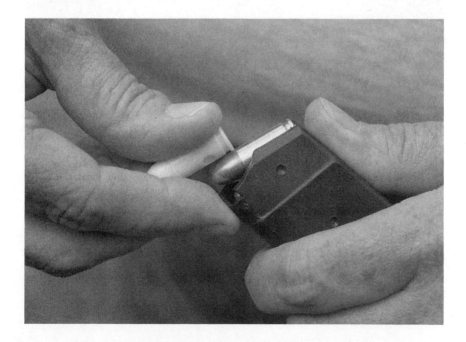

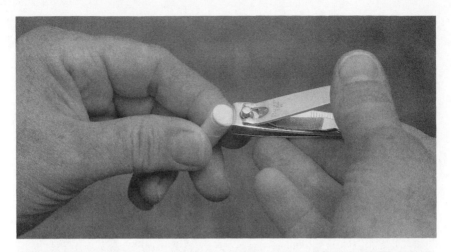

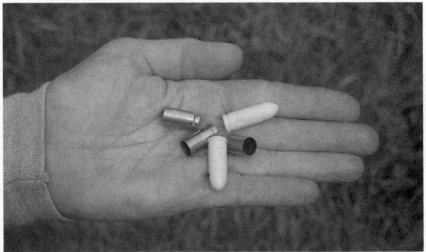

ter yet, have a trainer partner do it for you so you never know where they are.) Mix up the magazines so you can't anticipate what's going to happen, load a magazine into the gun, and start shooting any drill you'd like.

When you hit a stoppage, go through the steps of malfunction drill in order until you reach a point where the gun is up and running: TAP-RACK; if that doesn't work, RELOAD; if you can't reload the gun, perform a COMPLEX RELOAD (LOCK & RIP, RACK-RACK-RACK, RELOAD). The combination of fired brass and the modified dummy rounds will give you failures to fire, to load, to extract, and to eject. You won't be able to predict which will happen when, and you'll be forced to deal with the problems in this systematic manner.

CHAPTER 21

INTEGRITY IN TRAINING

Integrity (in teg ri te) - noun
1- *the quality of being honest*
2- *the state of being whole, unified, unimpaired, or sound in construction*
3- *internal consistency or lack of corruption*

In a way, this entire book is about integrity in training to survive a criminal attack: integrity in what you train, integrity in how you train, integrity in your practice, and integrity in you as a student.

Can you train without it? Certainly; many people do, every day. I don't believe that doing so leaves you in the best position to defend yourself, however, and I also believe that it wastes valuable training time. I shouldn't need to remind you, but your time on earth is limited. Why waste it?

HONESTY

Integrity demands that you be honest with yourself. Are you carrying your pistol because you actually have the determination to use it, if it is necessary and appropriate to do so? Or are you carrying it, as so many do, because you feel it keeps you safe but you'd never actually be able to drop the hammer on another human being?

It's the resolute attitude of the defender that makes her formidable; the pistol just makes her more efficient.

If you're not ready for the awesome responsibility and the possible consequences of using a handgun to defend yourself, be honest with yourself and don't carry it. To this day I run into new gun owners who bought a pistol under the mistaken belief that they can just wave it at their attacker and keep themselves safe. While it's true that the overwhelming majority of defensive gun uses do not involve actual shooting,[29] those instances where shooting is both warranted and necessary make it imperative that the gun's owner be emotionally and intellectually able to pull the trigger if it's necessary and warranted.

Massad Ayoob has famously said that criminals don't fear guns, they fear the resolute man or woman who is holding it. The source of that resoluteness is the defender's honesty with him or herself: that he or she really is willing to shoot if it becomes necessary to protect his or her life.

Commitment to training

You also need to be honest with yourself about your commitment to training and practice. Are you actually going to seek out training, or are you going to fall back on the "I've been around guns all my life, I don't need to take a class" excuse? The honesty part of integrity is what enables you to admit that you don't, in fact, know all you need to know simply because you had a .22 in the house when you were growing up. (The worst manifestation of this comes from those men who believe that they know everything they need to know about guns simply by virtue of possessing a penis. Sorry for the blunt and graphic comment, but it had to be said!)

Training can come in many forms. While attending a class is, I believe, the best way to train, it's not everyone that can attend a live class from a competent defensive shooting instructor. First, because not everyone who hangs out a teaching shingle is in fact competent, and second, because not everyone lives in proximity to a range where such training occurs.

It's possible to learn from books (like this one) and videos, but it will take longer, you'll make more mistakes, you won't have informed correction for

Not everyone can attend a class with a world-class instructor like Rob Pincus, but there are many alternatives to get good training. Start local!

your errors, and you might miss key points without even knowing. Learning from books and DVDs will take more dedication and attention on your part if you are to get maximum educational value.

Commitment to practice

Once you've gotten some training, are you honestly going to put in the practice time to build and maintain your skills? Defensive shooting skills are perishable; they need regular reinforcement through practice in order to remain usable. Practice also generates and maintains the recognition-recall links that are so important to expert-level decision making. Without a commitment to practice you won't retain the skills that you paid to acquire, nor will you be able to use them efficiently.

Your competency is your responsibility

Whether you're taking a class or learning on your own, your competency is up to you. The effort you put in, your dedication to understanding the concepts and your willingness to practice – not the parts that are fun but the stuff that's necessary – is what will build your competency.

When you go to a class, be a good student; have integrity. You're there, presumably, to learn something valuable. Pay attention to the instructor, strive to understand the concepts behind what he's telling you, and do what he asks. He may ask you to do something different than what you're used to doing; he may have a new method you've not been exposed to. If you reject it out of hand you'll not have the opportunity to develop competency. Do it his way; if after class you decide that it's not for you that's fine, but while you're there give it a fair shot.

The reason you train and practice is so that you can get better (more efficient) using the gun you'll actually be counting on to protect you. Discard anything, including your ego, which interferes with that.

At the same time you should insist that he explain why he's doing what he's doing. His explanations should be reasonable, plausible, and backed by objective data or deductions. If the explanation includes a reference to a famous soldier or police officer or competition shooter without a rational reasoning for the reference, you should ask questions about how it fits into your context. A good instructor should be able to give you the logic and detail to answer your questions.

Beware the instructor who says "try these different ways, and pick the one you like most." Defensive shooting techniques aren't about what you like, they're about what works well with the way attacks happen and with what your body does naturally. You're there to learn what the instructor believes is the best way to do that, and why he believes it to be. If all he does is tell you to pick your favorite, you can do that yourself without spending any money.

Am I saying that the instructor should have a "my way or the highway" approach? To a limited degree, yes. He should be professionally insistent that you put forth some effort to assimilate the techniques that he's teaching. You, on the other hand, should really put forth that effort without telling yourself that you don't like it or it's not like the method someone else taught you.

If the instructor asks you why you do something differently than he's asking, you should have an answer other than "that's the way I was taught." If that's the only answer you have, it means your last instructor didn't do a good job of explaining, or you didn't do a good job of listening. It may also mean that your way of doing things may not have a plausible reason for existence. If you find yourself saying "that's the way I was taught," it might be a sign that you need to pay more attention.

At the end of the course, if the instructor has done his job properly by explaining the plausible technique thoroughly and you've done your job by keeping an open mind, you'll have learned – really, truly learned – something new.

BEING WHOLE

The quality of being whole or of being sound means that the training and techniques you learn and practice really reflect and are applicable to your life outside of the range – your entire life, not just a piece here and there.

For instance, most people aren't going to do multi-floor house clearing of terrorists in their day-to-day lives. You can find lots of shooting courses, however, where you can spend a lot of time (and money) doing exactly that. If that's just not something that actually happens, why spend valuable time training for it?

Just about everyone plays several different roles in their lives. There's home, work, recreation, religious observances, and probably a bunch more I'm missing. In each of those roles there are plausible threats, and what is plausible may even change between them. If all you prepare for are the plausible threats in one single area of your life, the other areas may not be well covered.

Spending your scarce training resources doing things that have no plausible use, while ignoring plausible skills that might apply to the other areas of your life, isn't whole or sound.

This also applies to training with gear – including the gun and holster – other than what you can reasonably expect to use in a real attack. I see many people come to classes and train with full-size belt-carried guns but actually carry a small pocket gun on a day-to-day basis. (The worst offenders come to class with a big autoloading pistol on their belt but actually carry a five-shot revolver in their front pocket during the week!) Part of your integrity as a student is training and practicing with the gear you are actually going to carry.

Yes, I know that you shoot the bigger gun "better." Unless you're in that class or on the practice range to impress someone else, that's irrelevant. The reason you train and practice is so that you can get better (more efficient) using the gun you'll actually be counting on to protect you. Discard anything, including your ego, which interferes with that.

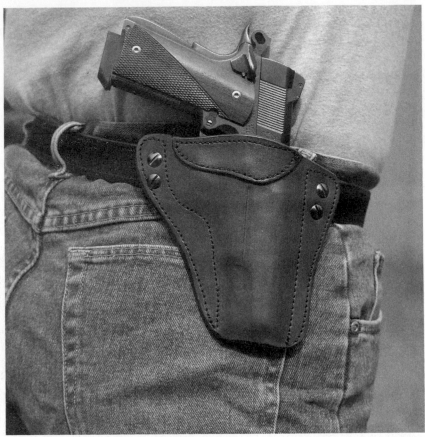

Carrying a 5-shot lightweight revolver in your pocket but practicing with a full-size autoloader on your hip isn't being realistic.

INTERNAL CONSISTENCY

In order for your training to have integrity it must be consistent, not just with itself but also with its expected use.

It's not terribly unusual to come across training doctrine which conflicts with itself at some level. When training is based on unrelated techniques that are chosen because they look cool or because some famous military unit used them, you'll often find that they don't work together well. I watched a video of a class where the students were taught to bring their guns up through a high ready position, much like I've described in previous chapters, when they drew their guns. When they did their version of an assessment after shooting, though, they dropped their guns down without bending their arms, into what has been derisively called the "urinal position." When they finished with their rather perfunctory assessment, they brought the guns back up into a high compressed ready, then holstered.

That's a lot of wasted movement and, for reasons we covered earlier, is neither consistent nor efficient. Their assessment was likely taken from one school of thought, while their draw stroke and ready position from another. The result was a conflict in action and a lack of internal consistency that resulted in a lot of wasted time and effort as well as lessened effectiveness.

Internal consistency means not just that the techniques don't conflict, but that they also work together to support an overall philosophy. Throughout this book I've talked about training in intuitive skills that are efficient under plausible circumstances; everything I've written, I hope, supports that overall view of defensive shooting.

"TOOLS FOR THE TOOLBOX"

There are things I could teach you that would be a lot of fun and look really cool in a video, but wouldn't really be applicable to any plausible scenario in your life. Yet, many people do teach such things and use the rubric "another tool for your toolbox" to justify it.

"Another tool for your toolbox" is a phrase that can mask a lack of plausible justification for a technique.

The whole concept of "tools for the toolbox" is often a smokescreen, a way to hide a lack of internal consistency. If the only justification for a technique is that it's another "tool," that's an indication that it might not have any application to any sort of plausible scenario, that's it's been included because the instructor is impressed with it for some unknown reason. (That, or he needs to make his students feel that they got their money's worth by "stuffing" the box full of useless tools.)

The toolbox metaphor is also a way for the instructor to avoid conflict; it's a cop-out. It may be that the technique actually does have a plausible reason for existence and that it's valuable to learn. There may be other people in the class, however, who cling to their existing technique because they have an emotional investment in it and won't be swayed by logic. If the instructor doesn't understand why what he's teaching is better and/or lacks the ability to articulate that in a way that allows the student to come to that understanding, then he might fall back on the toolbox analogy.

Whatever the reason, the "tools for your toolbox" comment should be seen as a red flag; an indication that there is little internal consistency or integrity in what's being presented.

Everything you learn needs to have a plausible application. If one exists, then there's no reason to bury it in a toolbox along with a lot of other implausible tools.

---

[29]Lott, John and Mustard, David, interview with Kris Osborne, Fox News. http://www.foxnews.com/story/0,2933,19857,00.html

CHAPTER 22

TRAINING IN CONTEXT

Perhaps the most important word in this book, as it relates to the what and how of your training, is the word context. As I mentioned earlier, context means the circumstances or conditions under which something can be fully understood or applied. It acknowledges that there is a relationship between a concept or idea and the specific kinds of situations in which it can be used (or for which it makes sense).

Understanding context is important because without it, it's easy to make bad decisions with regard to your training. Everything that you learn or practice has a context from which it came, and therefore a context in which it works and makes sense. If the context under which you're likely to use it doesn't match that where it originated, it's possible that it won't be as efficient (or even effective) as it should.

Something that works under one context often doesn't work well under another, but there are situations under which it might. Understanding the context in which you'll use it, as well as that of where it came from, is how you can decide whether it makes sense for your circumstances.

THE SHOOTING GAME CONTEXT

Competition shooting has been the source of a lot of innovation in the shooting world, innovation which has migrated to many other uses: hunting, military engagements, and even defensive shooting. That's not to say that the things done in the context of a game are universally applicable to defensive shooting, however.

Some of the advancements in competition shooting are context-neutral. For instance, competitive shooters helped develop the most efficient grasp for an autoloading pistol. For too long auto pistols were gripped the same as the revolver, and given their very different designs this meant that they weren't being used as efficiently as they could be. Competitive shooters, in their continual experimentation, found the thumbs-forward grip works best for autoloaders – and that is the grip that is overwhelmingly taught by defensive shooting instructors, including yours truly.

The closer a concept or technique gets to commonality between two contexts, the more likely it is to fit. For instance, the grip works in both competition shooting and defensive shooting because in both cases the shooter needs to control the gun while shooting rapid, multiple rounds; the need is the same, regardless of the environmental differences.

Other advancements aren't context-neutral. In the chapter on dealing with multiple threats, I showed you why the competitive "swinging transition" technique doesn't translate well to the defensive shooting world. The reason the transition technique doesn't work is because there is very little commonality between the two contexts. The environmental differences (live attackers versus static targets, surprise attack versus known and planned response, performance anxiety versus body's natural threat reactions) and the differences in goals (make good time at all costs versus survive the attack) all serve to make the techniques fail when crossed over.

Even something seemingly simple like using the sights suffers under the environmental variables. In a shooting match, even under the stress of the clock it's pretty hard not to be able to use your sights. In a defensive shooting, the visual changes due to your body's reactions make it physically less likely that you'll be able to use them. In the shooting match there's nothing to prevent you from using them; in the defensive shooting, your own body doesn't want to work that way. In the former you train to use the sights quickly, in defensive shooting you should train to use them only when you need to – with the default being not using them.

THE MILITARY/LAW ENFORCEMENT CONTEXT

While I have been a competitive shooter from time to time, I've never been in the military nor have I been a police officer. That means I'm in no way qualified to talk about how they do their jobs, nor am I qualified to evaluate their shooting techniques relative to those jobs.

Because I'm an avid student of and instructor in the means of surviving the criminal attack, however, I am somewhat qualified to evaluate how applicable their techniques are to private sector defensive shooting. This has been made possible by the large number of their alumni teaching in the private sector, and the material and techniques they're teaching becoming widely known as a result.

The jobs of those in the public sector (police/military) are different than those you and I have. For instance, in the military their job is to defeat the enemy and take ground (or, as some have pointed out, to kill people and break

Shooting while walking forward may have a law enforcement or military application, but for the rest of us just gives the bad guy more time to hurt us.

things). In law enforcement, the task is to apprehend the suspect (hopefully without casualties on either side). In those contexts, doing things like walking toward the enemy/suspect with the gun in a firing position might be a good way to do those jobs. Shooting while walking forward would be a task-related and thus needed skill.

In the private sector, I can't for the life of me imagine a plausible situation where I'd want or need to shoot at an attacker while walking toward him. This is a skill that public sector trainers often spend quite a bit of time when teaching private sector classes, even though it doesn't make a lot of sense in our context.

The same is true for shooting while walking backward. There may be some argument for it in their world (though I'm not sure what it would be), but again in the private sector it doesn't stand up to scrutiny: moving backwards slowly enough to be able to maintain a good balance of speed and precision doesn't really gain you much against someone with a contact weapon (knife/ club), as he'll be able to run toward you much faster than you can backpedal away from him. If he's armed with a gun, there is no physical way for you to move far enough backwards, fast enough, to significantly impact his ability to shoot you. Shooting while walking backwards is completely out of context in private sector self defense, and time spent learning to do it is largely wasted.

The idea that you can be ready or proactive is something that comes from a lot of law enforcement training. In their job, it makes sense: they get a call for a man with a knife, and as they head to the call they have the luxury of being able to think a bit about their response and steel themselves for what might happen. When they roll up on the scene they have the advantage of being able to get out of their vehicle while drawing their pistol, ready for action.

In the private sector, as I hope I've shown, the usual incident is a surprise. You don't have any of the luxuries of foreknowledge and must instead be able to respond without any sort of preliminary preparation, either mental or physical. Any technique or concept that relies on a proactive posture simply isn't a suitable or realistic way to train for the kind of threats we face (and drawing your gun only because you think you might need it is a good way to get arrested!).

GOOD TRAINERS, BAD TRAINERS

None of the foregoing is meant to denigrate the earnestness with which some of the competition shooters or public sector trainers present their material, nor to suggest that they aren't good at what they do. Some of them do understand the contextual difference between what they do in their "day job" and what their private citizen students need. Unfortunately, many more do not.

You need to examine what you're being taught and think about whether it's really applicable to the threats you're likely to face. Shooting while walking forward and backward, for instance, is a lot of fun to do and gives you a great feeling of accomplishment when you do it well. It even seems like they should be valuable skills, but when you sit down and analyze how attacks really happen in our world they suddenly don't seem all that important. That's because they aren't.

I've found that when someone tells me something outlandish is a "vital skill," what they often mean is that it's vital to something other than defending from a criminal ambush attack.

DEFENSIVE SHOOTING – IT'S MORE THAN MARKSMANSHIP

Some of the more experienced shooters in the audience probably just had a heart attack, but the fact remains that efficiently defending yourself from the criminal ambush attack isn't just about the shooting. It's about understanding what your reactions will be, learning to make decisions more efficiently, shooting well in relation to the target (as opposed to some arbitrary standard), using intuitive techniques, and so on.

Defensive shooting is about dealing with all the stuff your attacker is doing, all the stuff that you'll be doing naturally, and all of this in whatever environment you find yourself. You're going to have less control than most public sector trainers anticipate, and far less than the competition shooters can imagine. Train under the assumption that you're not going to have full control; if for some reason you find yourself in a situation where you have more control than you expected, you'll be ahead of the game!

CHAPTER 23

CHOOSING A TRAINING COURSE

It's possible to learn on your own, but it's better to do so under the watchful eye of a qualified instructor.

A s I mentioned in an earlier chapter, it's possible to learn defensive shooting skills on your own, but it's really not very practical. While defensive shooting is partly intellectual – knowing when to shoot and why to shoot – it is also mechanical and athletic, in the sense that you need to do physical things to be able to shoot.

A good defensive shooting instructor will give you a blend of both. He should be able to explain the need to process information before, during and after a shooting as well as how to draw the pistol efficiently and put the bullets where they need to go.

EXPERIENCE VERSUS ABILITY

There is a rather vocal subset of defensive shooting students (usually the "training junkie" type, those whose hobby is taking course after course) who proclaim they'd never take a class from someone who hasn't "seen the elephant." (That's a term meaning to have shot someone; they usually don't make a distinction under what conditions such shootings might have occurred.)

The problem with this attitude is that it's very difficult to find someone who has been involved in a sufficient number of truly defensive shootings from which to draw appropriate conclusions. I quoted Rory Miller at the beginning of this book as saying that fights are "idiosyncratic," meaning that they vary wildly in cause, execution, and conclusion. It's really not possible, except in the most generic sense, to derive a whole lot about defensive shooting from a single – or even two – events. A body of knowledge, of expertise, is only gained from being able to experience a sufficient number of events from which to distill similarities and lessons. That doesn't happen very often, if it ever has, in the realm of private sector defensive shootings.

Think of it this way: every so often you'll find a news report of a completely untrained person who prevailed using a firearm against a criminal despite making every mistake in the book. In other words, he got lucky (as the saying goes, luck counts but you can't count on luck).

By the "seen the elephant" standard, this guy would be well qualified to teach others how to defend themselves. Would I take a course from someone like that? No. Should you? I can't answer that other than to say it would depend on how much you value your own life.

The other way that your instructor can learn about defensive shooting is by studying defensive incidents carefully, looking for commonalities and deriving lessons from the mistakes and successes of others. Not having "dropped the hammer" on someone else doesn't preclude him from learning, for he has the experiences of a wide range of others from which to draw. As Simon ben Zoma said, "Who is wise? He who learns from all men." It's not so much the experience that matters, it's the ability to analyze the experiences of others that is truly valuable. The instructor who can do that brings not just a few experiences to teach from, but hundreds.

Ability to teach

In either case, whether from experience or study, the person who can teach is preferable to the person who can't. This is perhaps the most important quality a good instructor can have; no matter how expansive someone's knowledge, if he can't pass that on to his students in a manner that they understand then he might as well not have the knowledge in the first place.

A good instructor should first understand his material at its highest, most conceptual level. He must understand it so well that he can show you how to apply it in the widest range of circumstances. Even though he may only use 10% of that knowledge in any given class, each class may use a different 10%; if his knowledge doesn't go beyond that day's class he'll never be able to answer the questions from the next one. He is teaching beyond his knowledge level and his students will, sooner or later, move past his knowledge. At that point he either stops teaching or starts making things up as he goes along (and I've actually watched the latter happen).

Once he has a sufficiently high level of knowledge he must be able to articulate what he knows. He needs to be able to explain it to you in many different ways so that you can get a well-rounded feel for the ideas behind the techniques. An instructor whose command over the spoken language is poor is going to make a poor teacher, no matter how many times he's "seen the elephant."

IS BEING A GOOD SHOOTER A NECESSITY?

There is another subset of training junkies who insist that an instructor be a great shooter, and that he demonstrate his prowess before his students.

A demonstration may sometimes be the most efficient way to get an idea across to students. Language can be slow, but a visual illustration can be very fast. That doesn't relieve the need for the instructor to be able to articulate his

A demonstration can be a useful teaching tool, but it shouldn't be the primary one.

ideas, however; a demonstration should be the icing on the cake, not the cake itself.

Note that I never said anything about shooting! Off the top of my head I cannot think of a defensive shooting concept I teach which needs a shot for record (as opposed to a shot necessary to get the gun to operate, for instance to show how to reload from slide lock). Virtually all concepts and techniques can be shown dry, with nary a single shot being fired. Stance, grasp, and anything else that benefits from engaging the student's mirror neurons can be done without a single round of ammunition.

The instructor who relies on demonstrations of his prowess may not be giving his students the very deepest understanding of the material.

CONTEXT, AGAIN

I've talked quite a bit about context in this book, and picking your instructor or class is another instance where context becomes important.

If your instructor comes from a military, law enforcement, or competitive background it's important that he be teaching things that are really applicable for your day-to-day activities in your office. Just because he's achieved a certain rank, patrolled for a number of years, or won so many trophies doesn't mean that what he's teaching you, particularly if largely based on his own experience, is really applicable.

Again, knowing what's plausible in your life will help you weed out the useful from the useless. The techniques and concepts must match up to your life, must make sense in your environment; if they don't, it doesn't matter how much experience the instructor has. Don't for a minute allow yourself to believe that a uniform or a sponsor's t-shirt means anything to your life; think critically, ask questions, and most importantly expect answers.

THE CODE OF THE PROFESSIONAL DEFENSIVE SHOOTING INSTRUCTOR

There is a national organization of self defense firearms teachers, the Association of Defensive Shooting Instructors (ADSI), in whose birth I played a small role. It's composed of defensive shooting instructors from around the country, some famous and others who are only known to their students, who believe in the need for professional instruction in defensive shooting skills. They come together in the ADSI to share, learn, and advance the state of the art in defensive shooting education.

One of the requirements to belong to the ADSI is agreement with the Association's Seven Tenets – a code of behavior, of professionalism, which governs how the instructor teaches, interacts with his students, and relates to his counterparts in the rest of the industry. They're an indication of what the instructor believes and how he/she puts those beliefs into practice, and are what you should expect to find when you choose your instructor.

Tenet #1: *"I am committed to the safety of my students, and hold that the expected benefit of any training activity must significantly outweigh any known or perceived risk of that activity."*

We all know that shooting guns in a training environment involves some level of danger. We minimize our exposure to that danger – our risk level – by taking precautions. All safety rules should serve to reduce the risk of the activity, and your instructor should require that all the students follow them.

You as a student should require that your instructor carefully explain all of the safety rules, both the general ones and any specific rules or procedures for certain drills. If you don't feel that the benefits of that drill greatly outweigh the risks as you understand them, you need to ask for clarification. Maybe the instructor forgot something, or perhaps he didn't explain it well; no matter what the cause, he needs to live up to that commitment – and you need to hold him to it. Your life and health, and those of the students around you, depends on it.

Tenet #2: *"I believe that it is my responsibility to understand not just what I'm teaching, but WHY I'm teaching any technique or concept, or offering specific advice."*

It's been my experience that a lot of instructors don't really know why they're teaching or recommending something. It usually because they haven't spent a lot of time asking (and answering) probing questions about their material: is this relevant to the student's actual needs? Does it make sense? Is it supported by objective evidence? Is it consistent with everything else being taught? Can it be understood?

The right answer to any "why" question is "because it's the best thing for the students, and here are the rational reasons which support it." Every technique, every concept, every recommendation has to be considered by that measure. Your instructor should be able to answer the "why" as well (or better) than the "how."

Tenet #3: *"I recognize that defensive shooting skills, along with the drills and gear used, are inherently specialized and usually distinct from those of target shooting, competition and hunting endeavors."*

On the chapter about training in context I laid the groundwork for what should now be self-evident: the techniques used in defensive shooting are different than competitive shooting games.

It's not simply about being pro-competition or anti-competition. Your instructor needs to understand what, where, and why the differences occur, and be able to articulate them clearly if he/she is to give students what they need. This goes beyond the obvious stuff; it's necessary to understand the nuances, the seemingly little things that actually require big adjustments in curriculum. This only happens if the instructor isn't wedded to one point of view and if he/she really understands what defensive shooting is about.

Your instructor should demonstrate that he or she knows the difference, and can do that by acknowledging to you that there is a difference.

Tenet #4: *"I will encourage my students to ask questions about course material, and I will answer them with thorough and objective explanations."*

It's actually very easy to discourage students from asking questions. Think back to when you were in college: how eager were you to ask, in front of people you barely knew, what might be seen as a stupid question? Anything that a student perceives as being dismissive of their questions, or worse belittling of their state of knowledge, will put a damper not just on their desire for clarification but the rest of the students in class as well.

Every student needs to feel comfortable asking any pertinent question, and moreover it's important to always prompt for those questions. The students need to know that they can ask even the most probing questions about the material without being made to feel that they're unworthy.

Your instructor needs to give you answers that are complete and based on fact, logic, and reason. There should be a logical and plausible reason (preferably several) for every answer that's given, and they should all be factually based. Of course, they should also be consistent with the rest of his answers and curriculum.

You shouldn't accept flawed logic (like Appeal To Authority), unsupported conjecture, or incomplete/out of date evidence. Don't tolerate dogmatic sound bites that contain no fact and serve only to shut down further inquiry.

The professional gives students plenty of opportunity to ask questions. He maintains an atmosphere in which discourse about the topics is not only allowed, but encouraged on a continual basis (once at the end of class isn't enough). The answers to all questions are respectful of both the material and the student, and are based on provable and supportable facts – never mere opinions or sound bites.

Tenet #5: *"I understand that Integrity and Professionalism are subjective traits and I strive to maintain high levels of both. I am capable of, and willing to, articulate the reasons for the way I conduct my courses and how I interact with students & peers."*

Your instructor should always be above board; not just with you, but all of his other students and his peers. He needs to voluntarily be accountable to his students and his colleagues for everything he does. He should demonstrably adopt and behave to a high standard, and be open to constructive criticism, especially from you the student, when he comes up short.

Tenet #6: *"I believe that it is valuable to engage my peers in constructive conversation about differences in technique and concept, with the goal of mutual education and evolution."*

Being able to talk to other professionals about what he does, and finding out why they might do something different, is the basis of professional interaction. Every professional interaction I've had with other instructors has been an opportunity to learn, even when our approaches were quite different. In each of these I've come away with something that made me a better instructor, if only because it gave me an opportunity to advance my ability to articulate what I do.

How to tell if your instructor abides by this? Listen to him talk about other instructors; if he's throwing rocks or bad-mouthing others, he probably doesn't. There's a difference between respectfully or jokingly needling one's peers and talking trash about them. Professionals talk to each other; they don't throw rocks.

Tenet #7: *"I believe that the best instructor is an avid student, and I will strive to continually upgrade my own skills and knowledge. As part of this belief, I understand that my own teachings need to be subject to critique and open to evolution."*

Everything evolves, changes, progresses. It's how we as human beings make progress in any field – and defensive shooting is no exception. We've come a long way even in the last couple of decades, and I'm sure we'll move even further if for no other reason than to advance our teaching skills. The way the professional instructor does this is to be a student again.

Being an avid student doesn't mean signing up for another shooting class from a favorite guru, nor does it mean taking a class from someone whose curriculum is largely consistent with one's current worldview. It means seeking out new information and different approaches; being open and receptive to new ideas and giving them full (and honest) consideration; constantly striving to become a better teacher, as opposed to becoming a better shooter.

How to know if your instructor is really committed to advancing his knowledge? Ask him what he's changed his mind about in the last year: what does he teach now that he didn't twelve months ago, or what did he teach then that he doesn't now? Don't settle for a politician's deflection; if he's really learning and evolving, he should be able to tell you something specific that he either started or stopped teaching. This is really the litmus test for any instructor in any field.

FINAL THOUGHTS

This Code is a description of an ideal, a list of traits that other Professionals agree are desirable and laudable. It's not necessarily always achievable, but your instructor should always be working at it – and should be proud to tell you how he's doing so. There is always room for improvement, for progress, for evolution, and the Professional understands that. He doesn't stand still.

If you're a student of defensive shooting, it is what you should expect of your instructor. If you're an instructor, it comprises the things that you should want to do to better yourself, better serve your students, and move the industry as a whole forward.

CHAPTER 24

PRACTICING REALISTICALLY: DRILLS AND PROCEDURES

I n the chapter on making decisions more efficiently I talked about train-ing realistically, adopting techniques that were intuitive and thus realistic, and practicing under realistic conditions to the greatest degree possible. This chapter is about your practice: what you do after you've trained in the techniques I've outlined.

IT DOESN'T NEED TO BE AUTHENTIC TO BE REAL

In the training world we often use the term "realistic" to mean "authentic." For instance, many ranges or schools have shoot houses that are furnished much like your home might be. You'll find bedrooms, living rooms, and sometimes even offices (though I have yet to see a bathroom).

The concept is that if you train inside of spaces that resemble something in your world, the training is more realistic. The issue I have with this idea is that just because something looks real doesn't mean it's realistic. Unless it duplicates what your home is like, it's not realistic to you; it's just another abstraction but with better props. A much better word for these abstrac-tions is "authentic," in the sense that it looks like it could be an actual room somewhere, but it's not realistic because it doesn't represent a room which is familiar to you.

This isn't to say that abstractions are necessarily bad or to be avoided. An abstraction that represents your actual world is quite valuable, but one that represents someone else's probably won't be. The key is to consider your world and reproduce enough of it to get maximum value out of the exercise.

YOU NEED A PARTNER

Someone once asked me if I thought it was important to use a shot timer when practicing. I think I stunned the poor fellow when I told him I thought it was of little value; instead, I told him, the most important thing he could take to the range when practicing defensive shooting was a partner. (I think I further stunned him when I said that person doesn't even need to be a shooter!)

One of the biggest impediments to practicing realistically and developing your ability to use recognition like an expert is to be shooting the same thing all the time. You know what you'll be shooting, you know where it is, and you know what level of precision the target demands. There is nothing for you to recognize, which is one of the major points of practicing realistically.

Even using randomizers such as dice (throw the die then shoot the target whose number comes up) isn't enough because you have time to look at the die and figure out what you'll be shooting.

You need an unpredictable, random indication of the target to be shot. With each string of fire there must be options that you face, options which you must process before making the decision to shoot. The goal is to reduce your anticipation to the greatest degree possible. (We discussed the difference between readiness and anticipation earlier; you're on the range, you know you're going to be practicing, so it's foolish to believe that your readiness can be short-circuited. Your anticipation of the need to shoot, however, can be manipulated by your training partner.)

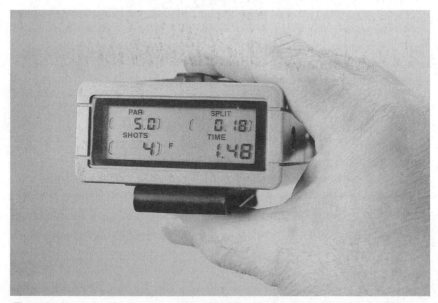

The author's vote for the most over-rated tool in defensive shooting training: the shot timer.

Your partner should be instructed to call different targets, varying in size, color, shape, distance, and whatever other variables you can introduce given the limits of the range and your equipment. Arrange to use numbers, letters, mathematical symbols, or even spelling challenges to force you to process information prior to executing your skills.

A random target call helps you develop your ability to recognize a threat, recognize the precision needed, recognize the balance of speed and precision which is appropriate to the circumstances, and to apply the correct amount of deviation control to deliver the accuracy needed. It helps you automate the response to the decision to shoot, allowing you to focus your cognitive abilities on the decision itself – just as it needs to be in an actual incident.

Don't shoot the same number of rounds each time!

Imagine this: in five minutes you'll be forced to shoot an attacker who is trying to kill you. How many rounds is it going to take to stop him?

If you answered anything other than "I don't know," you're fooling yourself. (If you answered "one, because I'm such a good shot/use such a powerful round," go to the back of the class and re-read every chapter from the beginning.) You don't know how many rounds it's going to take to cause your threat to stop, and you shouldn't be practicing as though you do know.

When you're practicing defensive shooting you should always practice firing a random number of shots that you choose (or better yet, visualize – more about that in a bit). Sometimes one, sometimes eight or ten – but most of the times you should shoot two, three, or four rounds. Don't shoot the same number twice in a row, and don't default to shooting the competition-inspired "double-tap."

TARGETS FOR DEFENSIVE SHOOTING PRACTICE

If someone folds a piece of paper in half and says "that's a good defensive group, and we're going to practice shooting it as fast as possible," that's not practicing realistically. You have nothing to recognize because the precision needed has been statically and arbitrarily predetermined. The drill becomes a choreographed and overly mechanical test of muscle control, and you end up focusing on the anticipation of the shot as opposed to the recognition of the need to shoot.

The ideal defensive shooting target isn't authentic, in the sense that it looks real (as with the photographic targets so popular these days). It is realistic, in the sense that you're not sure what needs to be shot (or even that there is something that needs to be shot) until your partner gives you some indication that you need to do so. This mimics the way that attacks actually happen: you're unlikely to know ahead of time what you're going to shoot, or even that you need to.

The I.C.E. Training Balance of Speed and Precision target from Law Enforcement Targets (www.letargets.com) is illustrative of the concept. In one target are four shapes, five colors, six numbers, three different sizes, two letters and several compass directions. On this one target your training partner can randomize the shooting calls to the point that you can't easily predict

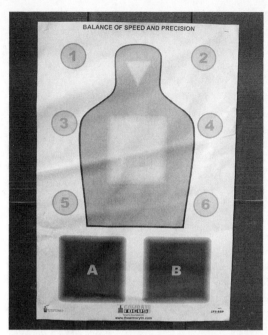

The Balance Of Speed and Precision target, available from Law Enforcement Targets, is an ideal training aid because of the number of ways in which it can be used.

what's coming next. In addition there are several targets that are duplicates, allowing you an easy way to practice the assess-and-respond approach to dealing with multiple attackers we talked about earlier. (The target is catalog #CFS-BSP.)

Don't think, however, that you need a fancy store-bought target to do these things. Here are some I printed out on my computer. Note the different sizes, shapes, and denominators. If you have a color printer (which I do) and live where it doesn't rain (which I don't) you can even make them in a variety of colors for added variables.

Still too fancy? Simple – use white paper and spray paint.

Spray paint can also augment an otherwise bland target to make it suitable for randomized practice calls. Take a blank IDPA or USPSA target and paint letters and numbers on it. Better yet, take several and mark them all up differently.

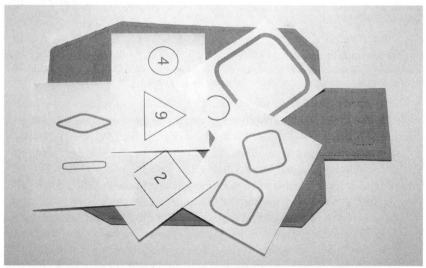

Almost any target can be used, and you can even make your own using simple shapes and your computer printer.

All you need for realistic training is some white paper, spray paint, and a little imagination.

It's easy to think that you need some special target to practice defensive shooting skills, but what you really need is imagination. In classes I use the I.C.E. target I showed above, simply because it's efficient in a class setting; we can go through a whole lot of drills before we need to change targets, which saves a lot of time. By yourself, though, that shouldn't be much of a concern and you can avail yourself of the more accessible options.

If you choose to make your own targets, either on your computer or just using spray paint, keep these guidelines in mind:

- You should have at least one target that approximates the size of the upper-center-chest of an attacker. An 8" circle works pretty well, as does a standard sheet of copier paper with the bottom 3" folded under.

- You should have at least a couple of shapes, and the more the merrier. A circle, triangle, and square are good for starters, and don't hesitate to turn the triangle in different directions.
- Vary the sizes. In general, the smaller targets should be no larger than half the size of the largest (the high-center-chest) target.
- Add numbers or letters (or both!) to some of the targets.
- If you can, adding colors gives you more options. Stick with the primary colors: black, blue, red, green. I've found that lighter colors like yellow don't show up well enough in many conditions.
- Don't add scoring areas. Remember that the target determines the precision needed; if you desire the chance to shoot with more precision, make the target smaller.
- Don't add "aiming points." Again, the target determines the precision needed; if you can't deliver that level of precision the aiming point isn't going to help, but more deviation control will.
- Don't worry about making perfect shapes or making them identical. This isn't a contest where everyone needs the same "fair" chance; this is practice at developing recognition and recall of shooting skills. You don't need perfect shapes for that.

VISUALIZATION AS REALITY

Visualizing a threat when you look at your target is a superb training tool.

There is a large body of evidence, which I'll leave to you to discover, which deals with visualization as a training and practice tool. The neuroscience is still being researched, but the general belief is that the brain doesn't really know the difference between what it sees and what it imagines.

This was brought home to me when my late father was in the hospital for a procedure and experienced a psychotic reaction to his pain medication. In his delirium he said he saw little men dropping wires out of the ceiling and climbing down onto his bed. He could describe the color coding of the wires (he was an engineer for the phone company – he knew his wiring!) and what the little men were wearing. As he told me afterward, they were perfectly realistic – as real as I was, he said. What the mind constructs is as real as what it actually sees.

You can use visualization as a tool to inject realism into your practice. Start by visualizing a threat when you look at the target. Visualize to whatever degree of detail you wish, but some of the variables to consider might be height, weight, sex, ethnicity, facial hair, shirt color, shoes, gloves, headwear, glasses, hair color, tattoos, eye color, jacket, vest, pants, shorts, pant color, shoelace color, rings or watches, and anything else you might think of.

The most important part is to visualize those clues that indicate to you that he is a threat: weapons (gun, knife, broken bottle, baseball bat, fencepost, motorcycle chain, screwdriver, etc.) and other indicators of intent like his actions, demeanor, facial expressions, and body language.

The key is to make it specific and don't repeat the same person. Make it different every time, lest you latch on to the idea that only "certain types" of people can be threats. Mix it up, but try hard to visualize to the extent that you see more than just your paper target.

Visualize effects

When you shoot, visualize your threat reacting to your shots; after you've fired whatever number of rounds you decide will defeat your attacker, visualize him or her falling to the ground, dropping the weapon, or giving up. This helps to reinforce the idea that you don't know how many rounds it will take to stop the attack until it happens, and it also helps to develop your ability to assess the threat as you shoot.

If you choose to visualize "follow the threat down," do so from a shooting position – don't relax!

Many people like to follow the target to the ground to ensure that he is really out of the fight. I have no problem with you doing this, provided your whole upper torso is involved. The gun should stay in and parallel to your line of sight as you follow the image of the target. If, however, all you're doing is dropping the gun into some sort of low ready position then don't. The idea of following the target is to be able to immediately trigger a shot if he proves to still be a threat; you can't do that efficiently if the gun isn't in a shooting position: in and parallel with your line of sight and fully extended.

If you choose to do this remember that the gun comes straight back into the high compressed ready when you're satisfied that he's down for good; from that position you start your assessment.

Visualizing an environment

A step up from the visualization of a threat is the visualization of space. Here you need to be specific. Visualize things from your life: your bedroom or living room, your office, your bank, the coffee shop you frequent, the mall where you go for your shoes, the parking lot at your favorite movie theater, or anyplace else that you've been and might likely be again. Don't forget your vehicles, your desk, or your spouse or children – those are all part of your world as well.

This is particularly important when doing drills, like dealing with multiple threats, in which the environment has a huge impact on what your attackers will do and how you will respond.

It's one thing to shoot a target on a static gravel range; it's another to see a vicious criminal in your local grocery store parking lot attack your wife while you're returning the shopping cart. The beauty of controlled visualization is that it allows you to practice your application of the skills you've learned in the context you'll likely use them. This is a huge aid to building the recognition-recall-response sequence we've been talking about throughout this book.

ARTIFICIAL LEVELS OF PRECISION

There is a practice/training strategy which you've no doubt encountered: the idea that you should shoot to a greater level of precision in practice because you'll shoot bigger groups in a real defensive encounter.

There isn't really a physical explanation for this conjecture. Several trainers – the most notable being Massad Ayoob – have experimented with injecting willing subjects of known shooting ability with epinephrine, then having them shoot a prescribed course of fire. In many cases the subjects shot just as well, or very nearly as well, as they did in their baseline tests. The muscle tremors and other effects of the reaction don't appear to dramatically affect the physical or athletic ability to shoot.

The goal is to make the connection between what you recognize and the skills you recall, and that doesn't happen without getting out of your comfort zone.

Students are often confused and reach a failure point when put through evaluations for which they haven't thoroughly trained.

Why, then, does the idea persist that you'll shoot at half the level of precision in an actual defensive encounter? I believe it's due to not training realistically – under the conditions you're likely to experience.

We often see it in classes when we put people through evaluation drills: exercises designed to test the student's ability to apply their skills in context. For a large percentage of the students, once we've stripped them of the anticipation of the need to shoot and randomize the target calls they tend to shoot with less precision than they do when shooting something familiar. Some of this is certainly performance anxiety, but much of it is simply because they haven't learned what their balance of speed and precision is under the circumstances which are being tested. They guess, and they often guess poorly. Once they get a good grasp of that their performance typically improves.

It all goes back to confidence in their skills: a large percentage of those students always shoot much more quickly than they can get the hits they need, and they tend not to alter their balance of speed and precision as their relationship to the target changes. They're over-confident because they haven't trained under realistic conditions sufficiently.

I see the opposite as well. Occasionally a student who has trained to shoot ever-smaller groups as a hallmark of defensive shooting will shoot far more slowly than he or she needs to during an evaluation drill. Unaccustomed to doing anything else, these students are under confident of their abilities; since all they have ever done is take their time to make "perfect" hits, that's what they do when presented with any shooting challenge.

You don't need to practice shooting to artificially or arbitrarily greater levels of precision to ensure that you'll be able to deliver a given level of precision on demand; you need to practice delivering an appropriate level of precision, dictated by the target and recognized by you, under varying and random conditions.

The goal is to make the connection between what you recognize and the skills you recall, and that doesn't happen without getting out of your comfort zone of always knowing what you're going to shoot next.

PRACTICE IDEAS

These are some suggested drills that are in accordance with the principles outlined in this book. None of them require more than a simple range (though drawing from the holster and the ability to "rapid fire" are necessary). Many of these are taken or adapted from drills taught to Combat Focus® Shooting students.

General concepts

When your training partner calls a target, any target, simulate the natural reactions you'll likely to encounter in a real attack: square your feet and body to the target, lower your center of gravity and lean forward (simply throwing your butt back 6"-8" will usually put you in the proper position), and start to bring your hands convulsively toward your line of sight as you look for your target. When you find it, start your draw stroke just as in the previous chapter: grip and move laterally (at right angles) to the target as you draw. You should be solidly planted – feet no longer moving – when you hit full extension and start shooting.

Don't choreograph your response; don't bring the hands up to a competition-like surrender position, for instance. I tell my students that the correct reaction to the command should look like a flinch – a strong, convulsive, somewhat exaggerated flinch that is different every time you do it. From that point the learned response of initiating the draw can begin.

You should not be drawing your pistol until you recognize that you have a verified target! Remember, train realistically: if you're in the mall and you hear a loud noise, are you going to immediately reach for your gun before finding out if there's really a threat? Of course not, but that's how most people train. Don't allow yourself to get into that competition-inspired frame of mind. Simulate the natural reactions, like the flinch, and only when you find your target and make the decision to shoot do you move laterally and draw your pistol.

Unless otherwise noted, the large (high-center-chest area target) is to be shot multiple times; make it a random number of rounds between 2-6. Mix them up and don't get into a pattern! The smaller targets (the numbered circles on the I.C.E. target pictured) are to be shot once, hit or miss. The misses give you valuable feedback as to your application of skill, and shouldn't be discounted – they're learning opportunities.

You should always be shooting as fast as you believe you can get the hits you need. If you're not getting the hits, slow down and apply more control

It's an extreme example – but if you haven't identified a target before drawing your gun, how do you know there's a target at all?

over your pistol! If, on the other hand, your groups are nice and small and centered in the middle of the target area, that's a sign that you're wasting time on meaningless increments of precision; speed up until you start missing.

Reload when you need to; your partner should not need to tell you to reload. When you recognize that you're out of ammunition, immediately reload the pistol. Remember to move when you reload – don't sit there like a target!

I suggest having at least three magazines on your person to maintain the momentum of the drills.

Balance Of Speed & Precision drill

Use a target with at a high-center-chest sized area and at least three smaller targets with numbers or letters in them. Your training partner should be told to make about 80% of the target calls on the large target; you can use any term you'd like, but "UP" and "THREAT" are simple and easy to understand even with amplified hearing protection. Occasionally he should call one of the small targets by number or letter.

The default for this drill is to focus on the target and keep your focus there. Simply bring the gun into and parallel with your line of sight and press the trigger. Later you'll make changes to this as you need to, but for now focus on the target and just bring the gun into your line of sight.

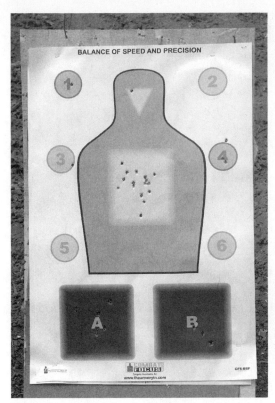

BALANCE OF SPEED AND PRECISION

Your partner should call a mix of large and small targets, and use colors, numbers or shapes to help randomize the commands.

Face the target from about three yards away. Have your partner call the target and you will respond appropriately (remember to simulate the body's natural reactions every time, including that natural shooting stance). As soon as you're finished, re-holster and wait for the next target command. Reload when you need to; do this until you run out of ammunition.

Now evaluate your target. Remember that accuracy is yes or no; you either hit within the target's area of precision or you didn't. Don't allow yourself to devolve into thinking that shots in the center are "better" than those that are off a bit. As long as they're inside of the target area, they're good – move on.

If you've got a nice group in the middle of the large target, you're taking too much time. Remember the discussion about shooting to a greater level of precision than the target requires? If you're doing that, speed up – take less time. Push yourself to the point that you start to land some shots outside of the target area.

Any shots that land outside of the target are misses; where are yours? On the large target, are the missed rounds on your first shot, or on subsequent shots? If on the first shot, it may be that your feet aren't planted when you start shooting, you're not at full extension, or your grasp is insufficient causing your trigger finger to steer the gun.

If the misses are on subsequent shots it's often a sign that you're not controlling recoil well. First correct any stance/grasp issues – make sure that you're not relaxing your grasp as the trigger resets and be certain that your center of gravity is lowered and your upper body weight is well forward (commonly called "leaning into the gun"). Be sure that your arms are extended as far as possible, preferably with your elbows locked, and that your shoulders are rolled up and forward. If those things don't solve your subsequent misses, then slow down! Slowing your shooting pace will usually bring those shots into the target area but should not be done until you've corrected any and all physical deficiencies.

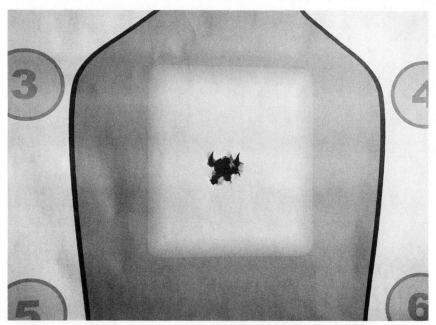

A tight group in the center of an area means you're taking far too much time for the level of precision the target dictates.

On the small targets you only have one shot; if you've missed, and you've corrected all of the physical issues I just talked about, it's possible that you need to use your sights at this distance and with that size target. On the next string of fire, use your sights if you feel you need to. If that corrected the problem, you now know that on targets of that size, at that distance, you need to use your sights.

Once you've done this several times (say, 70 rounds or so) move back to about five yards and start all over again. You might find that you don't need to use your sights at all at three yards, but at five yards you need to use them on the small

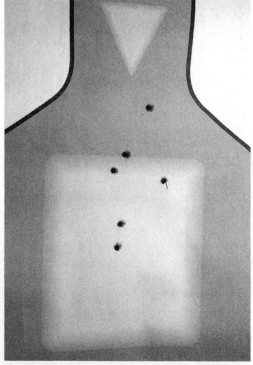

These misses came on subsequent shots, indicating the shooter doesn't have good control - or is simply shooting too fast to effectively control the recoil of the gun.

Repeated misses on a small target may mean you need to use your sights or work on your trigger control.

targets. That's fine! You'll likely find that you need to slow down a little bit at this distance; that's fine too. The reason you're doing these drills is to cement in your mind what balance of speed and precision you need for various targets at various distances.

You'll know that you've gotten a good feel for your balance of speed and distance at these ranges when you're always shooting as fast as you believe you can get the hits – and getting them. When you reach that point it's useful to extend your range just a bit, out to say seven yards. Again, start over and learn where your balance is at this distance. You'll find that you need to apply a lot more deviation control than you did up close, and that's going to slow you down. That's what you want to learn now, instead of when someone is shooting at you.

This is the basic drill that should account for at least half of your range time every time you practice. This isn't a drill that you shoot well and say "OK, I'm good at that!" It's a drill that's always changing, because your bal-

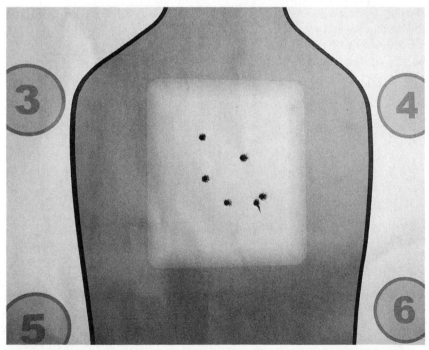

This target shows the shooter has a good grasp of his or her balance of speed and precision under specific conditions.

ance of speed and precision will always be changing. No matter how good yours is, it can always stand improvement!

Information Processing drill

Being able to process information prior to the execution of a learned skill is the basis of intuitive shooting. This drill tests your ability focus on something other than the shooting by giving you things you need to analyze before you can shoot.

For this drill you'll need the same sort of target as in the Balance Of Speed & Precision drill, but you'll need to have some additional options. (This is where the I.C.E. Training target really comes into its own, but again you can make perfectly suitable substitutes.)

You'll need a high-center-chest sized target and several smaller targets differentiated with numbers, letters, shapes or colors (preferably all of these). You can also have a second target stand with a similar but not identical setup – use different numbers, letters, colors or shapes on the second stand.

Your training partner's job is to mix things up for you. Just like the Balance of Speed and Precision drill, most of the calls should be on the high center chest area, but the rest of the calls should not necessarily be immediately obvious. For instance, he might use a math formula ("2 plus 3"!). He might say something like "what is the first letter of 'rabbit'?" (If he really wants to mess with you, he might call "what is the first letter of 'psychology'?" !) He can call a color or a shape, or a combination of the two (or anything else). If there is more than one target that contains the solution (two or more of

You can really increase the difficulty of information processing by adding numbers and letters to regular targets!

the same color, shape, or even number or letter) you'll need to go through a proper multiple threat assessment-and-response sequence.

Once or twice he should make a call for which there is no solution, just to test if you're drawing your pistol habitually rather than as a result of processing information. This drill is to develop your decision making and information gathering rather than just blasting away, and a no-solution call where you draw your gun reflexively should be met with criticism!

This is a drill that really benefits from video. Most people, when forced into thinking about stuff other than the actual shooting, start to revert back to well-trained routines that aren't necessarily intuitive. If, for instance, you've always trained in a bent-elbow Weaver stance and the neutral intuitive stance is relatively new to you, you're likely to revert back to old training when required to do something new – like thinking before shooting. Your training partner can help you with this, but if he or she isn't really up on the subject (or isn't a shooter) you won't get the feedback you need. Video is a wonderful tool to help you diagnose errors.

Moving Point Of Aim drill

This drill was taught to me by Georges Rahbani, a gifted instructor who also happens to be a good friend. It's an old drill, and I've heard it called by many names since first seeing it. (Rob Pincus, founder of I.C.E. Training, half-jokingly called it the "Dynamic Deviation Control drill" once, and the name stuck. It's actually a pretty good description!)

There are several goals of this drill. First is to impress upon you that no one holds a gun perfectly still, and that deviation control happens continuously as you shoot. It also, ironically, helps you to work on your trigger control by forcing you to think about something other than the trigger. For those who have developed a flinch, I've found this drill to be a quick cure. It teaches you to deliver whatever level of precision you need (based on what the target demands) and I find reasons to use it in nearly every class I teach.

Start with the large, high-center-chest sized area in the middle of the target. Your gun should be in your hands, extended in your line of sight and aligned in that area. Consciously – deliberately – move the gun randomly all over the area, being careful to keep in always within the confines of the box. Your finger will be on the trigger; as soon as your partner gives you the command to fire ("up!") immediately – without hesitation and regardless of where your gun is within the area – press the trigger promptly but smoothly. Recover and repeat until you've emptied the magazine.

If you've done this correctly, all of your shots will be within the target area. (On this large target it would be unusual for them to not be within the area!) The shots will probably be scattered within the box; if they're in a group in the center, either you got really lucky or you weren't actually firing immediately on command. If that's the case, redo the drill.

Now repeat the drill, this time using the next smaller target area. Let the gun move all it wants as long as it stays within the target area. The only difference is that now it will be moving a lot less. If you normally need to use your sights on this small target at whatever distance you're standing, use them.

Again, shoot immediately on command. If you have any shots outside of the target, which is likely to be the case, it's probably going to be due to one of the following: First, your trigger control might not be perfect and is steering the gun off of the target; you may have pressed the trigger much harder than necessary. Second, you may not be controlling the movement of the gun (insufficient deviation control) and allowed it to move outside of the target area. Third, you might be anticipating the shot and "grabbing" it when the command is given rather than simply pressing the trigger smoothly; this is usually due to an insufficiently strong grasp. Finally, your stance may be weak or less than solid. Consider each one of these, make any corrections you deem necessary, and shoot it again until all of your shots land inside the target.

Shooting to greater levels of precision (as dictated by the target) is simply a matter of reducing the amount of movement you allow the gun to make. You can use the smallest target or increase your distance to work on this idea, but don't go crazy – your goal is to shoot at plausible levels of precision at plausible distances. This drill is intended to teach you how to shoot to the level of precision that you need for whatever the target dictates. I shoot this drill at least once every practice session.

Volume Of Fire drill

A bad habit, particularly among competitive shooters, is always shooting "double taps." (I know there is constant debate on the difference between a double tap, a controlled pair, and a hammer; I use the term double tap to denote any two shots fired in extremely rapid succession.) If you're practicing that method now, it's important that you understand why it's a bad idea and how to break the habit.

First, as we covered previously you don't know how many rounds it's going to take to subdue your attacker. If your habit is to fire two shots then pause to fire another couple of shots, that pause is simply wasted time. It's not a lot, of course – perhaps a half second – but if you shoot six rounds in double taps that's a full second of time that you're not directly affecting your attacker's ability to mount a lethal threat.

Second, when I watch videos of actual attacks where many rounds are fired I don't see "bang-bang, bang-bang, bang-bang"; what I see is "bang-bangbangbangbangbang." The brain seems to know that pauses between shots serve no useful purpose and the result is typically a fast string of fire.

I've been criticized for saying this, but I think it's important to understand: the double tap is an admission to yourself that you can't control your gun in such a realistic string of fire. If you don't believe me, do this: go to the range and shoot your best double tap (fastest split time between shots). Now shoot at that same rate, but fire the whole magazine to the same level of precision that you shot the double tap. There are very few who can do that, and I'm willing to be that you're not one of them (don't worry - I'm not, either).

The double tap is a popular shooting cadence because it's how most of the shooting games are won: the fastest two shots that land in a target area. It's relatively easy to control the gun for two shots but it's a lot harder to do it for a string of fire, the kind that you'll probably be shooting when your life is on the line.

If you're likely to need to fire more than two shots to disable your attacker, but you can't put your third (or fourth or fifth) shot into the same target area as you did the first two, you'll need to slow down or you're going to miss.

The Volume Of Fire drill uses the large, high-center-chest area. Start at extension, with your finger on the trigger. Make sure you're in that natural, neutral stance and that you have the proper forward body weight posture; check your grasp and ensure that it's solid. On the command to fire, shoot the entire magazine at one consistent cadence that you know will result in 100% hit accountability. Don't speed up, slow down, or put pauses between your shots; the entire string of fire should sound like a metronome: bang-bang-bang-bang-bang-bang.

If you had a consistent cadence and all of your shots landed inside of the target area, repeat the drill but speed up a bit – say, 10% or so. If you still have 100% accuracy, speed up another 10%. Keep doing this until you have some misses. The last cadence at which you had perfect accuracy is your balance of speed and precision for that target at that distance at that point in time. You should now have the confidence to always shoot at that rate when under similar conditions as long as you apply the same level of skill (control) over the gun.

If you had some misses, correct any stance/posture/grasp/trigger control issues as we discussed above, then try again. If you still have missed shots, you now know that you can't control your gun at that cadence; slow down slightly until you have all your shots in the target.

I find that it's useful to shoot this drill at several plausible distances so that you get a very good feel for your balance of speed and precision at various ranges. It's also very important to shoot this with every pistol (or any other gun) that you expect to use for self defense, because you'll find that your cadence is different with different guns. That would be a useful thing to know before you really need to shoot.

My practice sessions usually start and often end with this drill.

PRACTICE WITH INTEGRITY

You will get out of your practice sessions only what you put into them. If you go to the range and shoot in one of the target-shooting stances or always use your sights because you "can," you won't get good results for defensive shooting purposes.

I'll admit that it's hard to always shoot from a natural, intuitive position (lowered center of gravity, forward weight bias). I've found it tempting to stand up straighter and use one of the relaxed competition shooting methods, but I also realize that's not how I'm likely to respond to the sudden ambush-like attack. I force myself to do it not because it's how I shoot my best, but because it's how I'm likely to shoot when I really need to.

Shooting in a way that's consistent with your body's natural reactions is tiring. It's better to practice less but in an intuitive way than it is to shoot more but with relaxed standards. If fifty rounds is all you can shoot before fatigue sets in, then limit your sessions to that number of rounds.

Over time you'll develop the stamina to extend the length of your practice, but don't succumb to peer pressure from the folks who brag about shooting hundreds of rounds each time they go to the range! In my never to be humble opinion it's better to practice properly but less than to practice poorly but more. Stay true to your goals, to yourself, and to the context in which you expect to need your pistol.

"I like to shoot competition, too – how should I practice?"

As I alluded to earlier, there was a time when I shot a lot of matches – IDPA, Steel Challenge, and Bianchi Cup-type competitions. I enjoyed it immensely, particularly the Steel Challenge type matches – there's something terribly addictive about that 'CLANG'!

Despite my love of competition, I gave it up largely because of my recognition that there is a difference between defensive shooting and competition shooting. That's not to say that they can't co-exist, but you will need to come to grips with the fact that those differences will affect your practice.

What is the proper balance in training and practice between them? Go back and re-read the drill about cognitive decision making. The reason we do that drill is to get ourselves to think about something other than the drawing and shooting. Our goal is to develop the recognition/recall patterns thoroughly enough that once the decision to shoot has been made, there is no need to think about the mechanics. We want the execution of our intuitive skills to be automated, and practice routines like that drill help us do that.

You'll know that the proper balance between competitive and defensive practice has been reached when you have to think about how to shoot competitively, but you don't have to think about how to shoot defensively.

What do I mean by that? When you're standing in the shooting box at a match, waiting for the buzzer to go off, if you have to consciously think about using something other than a natural, instinctive crouch; if you have to think about using your sights; if you have to think about doing your reloads the fastest way, not the most error-resistant way; if you have to think about shooting only double-taps instead of realistic strings of fire and so on, you have the proper bias toward defensive shooting.

An improper balance between those worlds occurs when you have to do the opposite: you have to think about using intuitive skills when practicing your defensive shooting. If you find yourself in defensive shooting practice having to remember to use a natural, neutral stance; if you have to think about doing your reloads efficiently, out of your line of sight so that you can focus on the threat; if you have to think about not choreographing your strings of fire – among the many other things we've covered – then you have a balance that's biased toward competition.

Does this mean your competition shooting will probably suffer? In most cases, it probably does. This brings us back to that integrity discussion: are you more interested in being an efficient defensive shooter, or a faster competitive shooter? Your answer will guide your decisions, but don't fool yourself: they are two different contexts and are quite difficult to reconcile to high standards in both.

Understand the decisions you make, why you're making them, and have the courage to stand by them.

RESPECTFUL IRREVERENCE

Rob Pincus wrote this piece some years ago, and it was in fact responsible for our first meeting. I read it online where it's been widely quoted, and was impressed enough to contact him and thank him for writing it.

The shooting world is full of hero worship. I have no issue with holding someone in great esteem, but if we're not careful to separate the man from his material we risk stifling our evolution. This essay is about maintaining the correct balance between admiration and deification, and I thank Rob for allowing me to reprint it here.

RESPECTFUL IRREVERENCE
by Rob Pincus

When any person, idea, technique, school, piece of gear, team or tactic is put on a pedestal, we risk stopping progress. We should all be trying to constantly improve our own ability to achieve our goals as efficiently as possible. In the defensive/tactical world, that means becoming more dangerous to our enemies and better prepared to deal with violent conflicts. If, at any point, we decide that someone or something is beyond being questioned we will limit our ability to improve. History is full of revered truths and experts that turned out to be wrong. Acknowledging this simple fact should remind us that today's experts and truths may be just as vulnerable to improvement.

Being open to questioning those who would be experts does not mean disrespecting them. In fact, if we look hard enough, we will probably find that our heroes themselves challenged a previously held belief or expert in order to develop their own conclusions and truths. This process is necessary for progress. I don't think anyone in the training industry has less than outstanding intentions. As instructors, however, we are all limited by the exposure we have to ideas and our ability to process them. We are limited by the type of students we have worked with, the facilities at which we've taught and the systems in which we operate.

It has been said that a 3rd year college physics major today knows more about the relationship between matter and energy than Albert Einstein did when he wrote the Theory of Relativity which describes it. In a perfect world, the students will always eventually outshine the instructors. I know that I have learned a lot from students and their feedback. Student questions have forced me to examine my own teachings more closely and sometimes change them for the better. Occasionally, feedback from students (including those who watch instructional DVDs or read articles like this one) can turn an idea on its ear and initiate a whole new approach to a problem or explanation for a solution.

I have spent a lot time over the last few years doing instructor development for civilian, military and law enforcement personnel. I want to take this opportunity to share with the readers of this article some of the important tenets that I pass on during those courses that I think benefit us as students as well in our approach to training.

Success Breeds Complacency

We learn from mistakes and improve through failure. Success breeds only complacency and pride. While we love to celebrate our victories, we need to spend much more time analyzing our losses in order to find areas to improve. Training that revolves around ego building and developing a positive mental attitude tends to become a choreographed series of feel-good-drills and simplistic scenarios.The fact that some technique has been used successfully does not mean that it is unquestionable. History is full of examples of "best ways" that were bested through innovation, experimentation and critical thinking.

Avoid Absolutes

Never say Never. Skepticism is an important trait in anyone seeking to improve on an existing system. Without a fair dose of skepticism, one is likely to jump on the first bandwagon that passes by. Once on-board, a failure to think critically can lead to figuratively being taken for a ride. One of the first indications of a need for questions is an absolute. If someone says "Always" or "Never", it is your responsibility to find the exception. By identifying the exception, you will improve the system and be able to better prepare. If the exception doesn't exist... look again, or be open to accepting it (and adjusting appropriately) if someone else finds it.

Ask (and Answer) the "Why?" Questions

"Just another tool for your toolbox" is potentially the single most damaging phrase in the training industry. Instructors owe their students more of an explanation for investing time & effort (let alone money) in a technique, tactic or principle than to just offer that it is something that might work for them. Most instructors use this phrase not out of ignorance; they use it to avoid confrontations with Type A students who might want to argue based on previous training, or they use it out of their own complacency because it has never been questioned, or they might use it because they truly believe that the tactic is simply just another tool. I think the student deserves a detailed explanation as to why the instructor is teaching any given skill or concept. Intellectual Comfort with an idea is vital to efficient learning. If the answer to the "Why?" question is "…because that's how [we/the team/some other team/ this school/etc] does it!" I really suggest a long & hard deep breath, followed by extreme skepticism throughout the rest of the course. Dogma has no place in this arena. My staff instructors operate under threat of termination if they ever use this type of answer with a student. An instructor should always teach what they truly believe to be the best option for any given situation and be ready, willing and able to explain why.

Context dictates Curriculum

Students should be taught things that will work in the context that they are likely to need them. Spouting content blindly without regard for the realities of the student is simply lecturing, not teaching. Picture the guy who stands in front of a power-point and reads it to the class. Unfortunately, this type of "instructor" is far too common and sometimes offers little to the student. Any course outline needs to be open to adjustment to accommodate the student situations, questions, equipment and abilities. I always say that I know about 95% of what I'm going to teach at the start of any given course, the last 5% comes from student interactions and it is often some very important stuff! If you follow these four principles as often as possible, and look for instructors who do as well, you should be able to get more out of your training time and effort.

Avoiding complacency and absolutes, answering the "Why?" questions and allowing context to influence curriculum whenever you can, may not be easy. It might even bruise some egos… maybe even yours. If the attitudes of those involved are properly aimed at the goal of improving without regard for personal preferences, the irreverence does not have to be disrespectful. We should all be standing on the shoulders of the giants that have come before us in the training industry, which enables us to see farther and reach higher than they did. If we instead kneel at the feet of those giants, be they people, schools or organizations, we will fail to build on what they have established and stagnate. The dictionary defines 'irreverent' as 'lacking in respect', or 'impious'. I prefer the latter definition in this case and believe that it is possible to be respectful of people while still not worshipping any one source of information.

In short, the next time you think about your preferred source of tactical wisdom or technical expertise: Honor the men, challenge the material.

AN ALTERNATE LOOK AT HANDGUN STOPPING POWER

By Greg Ellifritz

I've been interested in firearm stopping power for a very long time. I remember reading Handguns magazine back in the late 1980s when Evan Marshall was writing articles about his stopping power studies. When Marshall's first book came out in 1992, I ordered it immediately, despite the fact that I was a college student and really couldn't afford the $39 price tag. Over the years I bought all of the rest of Marshall's books as well as anything else I could find on the subject. I even have a first edition of Gunshot Injuries by Louis Lagarde published in 1915.

Every source I read has different recommendations. Some say Marshall's data is genius. Some say it is statistically impossible. Some like big heavy bullets. Some like lighter, faster bullets. There isn't any consensus. The more I read, the more confused I get.

I had a problem with the methodology of Marshall and Sanow's work. For consistency purposes, they ONLY included hits to the torso and ONLY included cases where the person was hit with just a single round. They excluded all shootings where a person was hit with more than one round. This lead to an unrealistically high stopping power percentage, because it factored out the majority of the cases when a person didn't stop!

Massad Ayoob, when writing about his own stopping power studies, suggested that if people didn't believe his data or anyone else's, they should do a study of their own. That seemed like good advice to me. So I started collecting data.

Over a 10-year period, I kept track of stopping power results from every shooting I could find. I talked to the participants of gunfights, read police reports, attended autopsies, and scoured the newspapers, magazines, and Internet for any reliable accounts of what happened to the human body when it was shot.

I documented all of the data I could; tracking caliber, type of bullet (if known), where the bullet hit and whether or not the person was incapacitated. I also tracked fatalities, noting which bullets were more likely to kill and which were not. I looked at hits to different parts of the body and explored what happened when people were shot multiple times. It was an exhaustive project undertaken during my spare time as I worked as a full time police firearms instructor and obtained a graduate degree.

Before I get to the details, I must give a warning. I'm not tied to the results of my study. Many of the results surprised me! I don't sell ammo. I'm not being paid by any firearm or ammunition manufacturer. I carry a lot of different pistols for self defense. I 'm just reporting the data I gathered. If you don't like it, take Mr. Ayoob's advice and do a study of your own.

Here's what I looked at:
• Number of people shot
• Number of rounds that hit
• On average, how many rounds did it take for the person to stop his violent action or be incapacitated? For this number, I included hits anywhere on the body. To be considered an immediate incapacitation, I used criteria similar to Marshall's. If the attacker was striking or shooting the victim, the round needed to immediately stop the attack without another blow being thrown or shot being fired. If the person shot was in the act of running (either towards or away from the shooter), he must have fallen to the ground within five feet. I also excluded all cases of accidental shootings or suicides. Every shot in this study took place during a military battle or an altercation with a criminal.
• What percentage of shooting incidents resulted in fatalities. For this, I included only hits to the head or torso.
• What percentage of people were not incapacitated no matter how many rounds hit them
• Percentage of people who were immediately stopped with one hit to the head or torso

Here are the results:

.22 (short, long and long rifle)
  # of people shot- 154
  # of hits- 213
  % of hits that were fatal- 34%
  Average number of rounds until incapacitation- 1.38
  % of people who were not incapacitated- 31%
  % actually incapacitated by one shot (torso or head hit)- 60%

.25ACP-
  # of people shot- 68
  # of hits- 150
  % of hits that were fatal- 25%
  Average number of rounds until incapacitation- 2.2
  % of people who were not incapacitated- 35%
  % actually incapacitated by one shot (torso or head hit)- 49%

.32 (both .32 Long and .32 ACP)
  # of people shot- 25
  # of hits- 38
  % of hits that were fatal- 21%
  Average number of rounds until incapacitation- 1.52
  % of people who were not incapacitated- 24%
  % actually incapacitated by one shot (torso or head hit)- 72%

.380 ACP
  # of people shot- 85
  # of hits- 150
  % of hits that were fatal- 29%
  Average number of rounds until incapacitation- 1.76
  % of people who were not incapacitated- 16%
  % actually incapacitated by one shot (torso or head hit)- 62%

.38 Special
  # of people shot- 199
  # of hits- 373
  % of hits that were fatal- 29%
  Average number of rounds until incapacitation- 1.87
  % of people who were not incapacitated- 17%
  % actually incapacitated by one shot (torso or head hit)- 55%

9mm Luger
  # of people shot- 456
  # of hits- 1121
  % of hits that were fatal- 24%
  Average number of rounds until incapacitation- 2.45
  % of people who were not incapacitated- 13%
  % actually incapacitated by one shot (torso or head hit)- 47%

.357 (both Magnum and Sig)
  # of people shot- 105
  # of hits- 179
  % of hits that were fatal- 34%
  Average number of rounds until incapacitation- 1.7
  % of people who were not incapacitated- 9%
  % actually incapacitated by one shot (torso or head hit)- 61%

40 S&W
   # of people shot- 188
   # of hits- 443
   % of hits that were fatal- 25%
   Average number of rounds until incapacitation- 2.36
   % of people who were not incapacitated- 13%
   % actually incapacitated by one shot (torso or head hit)- 52%

.45 ACP
   # of people shot- 209
   # of hits- 436
   % of hits that were fatal- 29%
   Average number of rounds until incapacitation- 2.08
   % of people who were not incapacitated- 14%
   % actually incapacitated by one shot (torso or head hit)- 51%

.44 Magnum
   # of people shot- 24
   # of hits- 41
   % of hits that were fatal- 26%
   Average number of rounds until incapacitation- 1.71
   % of people who were not incapacitated- 13%
   % actually incapacitated by one shot (torso or head hit)- 53%

Rifle (all Centerfire)
   # of people shot- 126
   # of hits- 176
   % of hits that were fatal- 68%
   Average number of rounds until incapacitation- 1.4
   % of people who were not incapacitated- 9%
   % actually incapacitated by one shot (torso or head hit)- 80%

Shotgun (All shotgun rounds included, but 90% of results were from 12 gauge)
   # of people shot- 146
   # of hits- 178
   % of hits that were fatal- 65%
   Average number of rounds until incapacitation- 1.22
   % of people who were not incapacitated- 12%
   % actually incapacitated by one shot (torso or head hit)- 86%

DISCUSSION

I really would have liked to break it down by individual bullet type, but I didn't have enough data points to reach a level of statistical significance. Getting accurate data on nearly 1800 shootings was hard work. I couldn't imagine breaking it down farther than what I did here. I also believe the data for the .25, .32 and .44 magnum should be viewed with suspicion. I simply don't have enough data (in comparison to the other calibers) to draw an accurate comparison. I reported the data

I have, but I really don't believe that a .32 ACP incapacitates people at a higher rate than the .45 ACP!

One other thing to look at is the 9mm data. A huge number (over half) of 9mm shootings involved ball ammo. I think that skewed the results of the study in a negative manner. One can reasonable expect that FMJ ammo will not stop as well as a state of the art expanding bullet. I personally believe that the 9mm is a better stopper than the numbers here indicate, but you can make that decision for yourself based on the data presented.

Some interesting findings:

I think the most interesting statistic is the percentage of people who stopped with one shot to the torso or head. There wasn't much variation between calibers. Between the most common defensive calibers (.38, 9mm, .40, and .45) there was a spread of only eight percentage points. No matter what gun you are shooting, you can only expect a little more than half of the people you shoot to be immediately incapacitated by your first hit.

The average number of rounds until incapacitation was also remarkably similar between calibers. All the common defensive calibers required around 2 rounds on average to incapacitate. Something else to look at here is the question of how fast can the rounds be fired out of each gun. The .38 SPL probably has the slowest rate of fire (long double action revolver trigger pulls and stout recoil in small revolvers) and the fewest rounds fired to get an incapacitation (1.87). Conversely the 9mm can probably be fired fastest of the common calibers and it had the most rounds fired to get an incapacitation (2.45). The .40 (2.36) and the .45 (2.08) split the difference. It is my personal belief that there really isn't much difference between each of these calibers. It is only the fact that some guns can be fired faster than others that causes the perceived difference in stopping power. If a person takes an average of 5 seconds to stop after being hit, the defender who shoots a lighter recoiling gun can get more hits in that time period. It could be that fewer rounds would have stopped the attacker (given enough time) but the ability to fire more quickly resulted in more hits being put onto the attacker. It may not have anything to do with the stopping power of the round.

Another data piece that leads me to believe that the majority of commonly carried defensive rounds are similar in stopping power is the fact that all four have very similar failure rates. If you look at the percentage of shootings that did not result in incapacitation, the numbers are almost identical. The .38, 9mm, .40, and .45 all had failure rates of between 13% and 17%.

Some people will look at this data and say "He's telling us all to carry .22s". That's not true. Although this study showed that the percentages of people stopped with one shot are similar between almost all handgun cartridges, there's more to the story. Take a look at two numbers: the percentage of people who did not stop (no matter how many rounds were fired into them) and the one-shot-stop percentage. The lower caliber rounds (.22, .25, .32) had a failure rate that was roughly double that of the higher caliber rounds. The one-shot-stop percentage (where I considered all hits, anywhere on the body) trended generally higher as the round gets more powerful. This tells us a couple of things...

In a certain (fairly high) percentage of shootings, people stop their aggressive actions after being hit with one round regardless of caliber or shot placement. These people are likely NOT physically incapacitated by the bullet. They just don't want to be shot anymore and give up! Call it a psychological stop if you will. Any bullet or caliber combination will likely yield similar results in those cases. And fortunately for us, there are a lot of these "psychological stops" occurring. The problem we have is when we don't get a psychological stop. If our attacker fights through the pain and continues to victimize us, we might want a round that causes the most damage possible. In essence, we are relying on a "physical stop" rather than a "psychological" one. In order to physically force someone to stop their violent actions we need to either hit him in the Central Nervous System (brain or upper spine) or cause enough bleeding that he becomes unconscious. The more powerful rounds look to be better at doing this.

One other factor to consider is that the majority of these shootings did NOT involve shooting through intermediate barriers, cover or heavy clothing. If you anticipate having to do this in your life (i.e. you are a police officer and may have to shoot someone in a car), again, I would lean towards the larger or more powerful rounds.

What I believe that my numbers show is that in the majority of shootings, the person shot merely gives up without being truly incapacitated by the bullet. In such an event, almost any bullet will perform admirably. If you want to be prepared to deal with someone who won't give up so easily, or you want to be able to have good performance even after shooting through an intermediate barrier, I would skip carrying the "mouse gun" .22s, .25s and .32s.

Now compare the numbers of the handgun calibers with the numbers generated by the rifles and shotguns. For me there really isn't a stopping power debate. All handguns suck! If you want to stop someone, use a rifle or shotgun!

What matters even more than caliber is shot placement. Across all calibers, if you break down the incapacitations based on where the bullet hit you will see some useful information.

Head shots = 75% immediate incapacitation

Torso shots = 41% immediate incapacitation

Extremity shots (arms and legs) = 14% immediate incapacitation.

No matter which caliber you use, you have to hit something important in order to stop someone!

CONCLUSION

This study took me a long time and a lot of effort to complete. Despite the work it took, I'm glad I did it. The results I got from the study lead me to believe that there really isn't that much difference between most defensive handgun rounds and calibers. None is a death ray, but most work adequately... even the lowly .22s. I've stopped worrying about trying to find the "ultimate" bullet. There isn't one. And I've stopped feeling the need to strap on my .45 every time I leave the house out of fear that my 9mm doesn't have enough "stopping power". Folks, carry what you want. Caliber really isn't all that important.

Take a look at the data. I hope it helps you decide what weapon to carry. No matter which gun you choose, pick one that is reliable and train with it until you can get fast accurate hits. Nothing beyond that really matters!

Greg Ellifritz is the full time firearms and defensive tactics training officer for a central Ohio police department. He holds instructor or master instructor certifications in more than 75 different weapon systems, defensive tactics programs and police specialty areas. Greg also has a master's degree in Public Policy and Management and is an instructor for both the Ohio Peace Officer's Training Academy and the Tactical Defense Institute. He can be reached at Greg1095@yahoo.com or his website, http://www.activeresponse-training.net

ABOUT THE AUTHOR

GRANT CUNNINGHAM is a renowned author and teacher specializing in personal security and defensive shooting topics. His emphasis is on preparing ordinary citizens to efficiently deal with extraordinary circumstances, teaching "real skills, for real people, living real lives."

In addition to his books, Grant's articles on shooting and self defense have been published in a number of popular magazines and on websites like Personal Defense Network. He is a founding member and former Executive V.P. of the Association of Defensive Shooting Instructors, the nationwide professional membership organization for those who teach the use of firearms for self defense.

Known for his thorough, factual, yet highly engaging instructional style, Grant teaches frequently at locations around the U.S. You can find out more about Grant, his courses, and his available class dates through his websites: www.personalsecurity.us and www.grantcunningham.com.

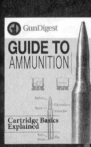
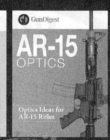
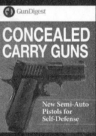

IMPROVE YOUR SHOOTING SKILLS

Handgun Training for Personal Protection is a must-read for anyone who is serious about maximizing their self-defense skills. This latest title from handgun authority Richard A. Mann teaches you how to get the most from your training.

" This book belongs in every shooter's library. Mann provides a practical, hands-on guide to working with your handgun and the equipment that goes with it. Along the way, common misconceptions are corrected, and often neglected topics are explained. This book will become your go-to reference. "

—**Il Ling New,** *Gunsite Instructor*

HANDGUN TRAINING
FOR PERSONAL PROTECTION

Richard A. Mann

How To Choose & Use The Best Sights, Lights, Lasers & Ammunition

3 EASY WAYS TO ORDER

www.gundigeststore.com
(product U2147)

Download to your Kindle,
Nook or iPad tablet

Call (855) 840-5120
(M-F, 8-5 CST)